Historical Infrastructure

of the

Virginia Military Institute

and Related Biographies

by

Danny Hogan

The author for this book, Danny Andrew Hogan was born in Roanoke, Virginia in 1943, graduated from the Jefferson Senior High School in 1961, and was captain of the Bravo Company in the VMI Class of 1965. After graduation from VMI, he joined the U.S. Air Force (USAF) and earned his pilot's license. In 1970, he graduated from the University of Southern California with a Master of Science degree for research and development for systems management. As a result, he developed plans and budgets for the USAF in the Pentagon from 1973 to 2003. In 1975, he switched from an active USAF member to a reservist, and joined the U.S. Commerce Department following the VMI "citizen-soldier" path. Most of his federal employment was in the U.S. Department of Energy (DoE) from 1977 until he retired in 1996. His jobs included the DoE deputy Chief Financial Officer, deputy director of the office of Naval Petroleum and Oil Shales Reserves, and manager of the large Elk Hills oilfield in California (1988-1996). At DoE he was a Senior Executive Service person and retired from the U.S. Air Force as a Major General in 2003.

First Printing

Copyright © 2019

Author
Danny Hogan

Cover and manuscript graphic design

Publisher
Wayne Dementi
Dementi Milestone Publishing
Manakin-Sabot, VA 23103
www.dementimilestonepublishing.com

ISBN
978-1-7325179-7-4

Library of Congress Control Number: 2019932661

Printed in the USA

DEDICATION

This book is dedicated to

VMI Alumni and Cadets

CONTENTS

Preface

The idea for this book originated in 2015 at my 50th VMI Reunion. I was primarily curious about the men whose names were used for the buildings and statues on the Post, but could find only minimal history about them. My first plan was a simple guide-map to briefly describe the VMI infrastructure and biographies. After discovering a lot of information including pictures, the brief guide-map objective converted to writing a book with four sections addressing historical background for the buildings, the residences, the athletic facilities, and the many statues, arches, monuments, and memorials on the VMI Post. Also included are histories of the men for whom the infrastructures were named and recognition of the principal architects A.J. Davis and Bertram Goodhue who guided VMI's outstanding appearance that led to a National Historic District.

After my reunion, I contacted Colonel Keith Gibson (VMI Class of 1977), the director of the VMI Museum, and *de facto* architectural historian of the Institute. Col. Gibson recommended a number of avenues of research, starting with a 2007 report, "*Preservation Master Plan for the Virginia Military Institute*", a comprehensive document by the Pennsylvania architectural preservation firm, John Milner Architects. (A Getty Foundation grant funded the Milner project.)

Col. Gibson also directed me to Colonel Diane Jacob, the VMI archivist, who outlined for me the vast amount of digital information available in Preston Library—a trove of VMI pictures and articles from Institute Reports, as well as cadet newspapers, yearbooks, and minutes of the Board of Visitors. Website sources Google.com and Ancestry.com were also very helpful in ascertaining accurate biographical information about individuals.

In the course of my research, a number of books surfaced (listed in the bibliography) which were especially important, most notably "*One Hundred Years at V.M.I.*", a four-volume, 1600-page history of the Institute by Colonel William Couper (1884-1964), a member of the Class of 1904 and VMI Executive Officer and Historiographer between 1925 and 1954.

I am deeply grateful to Col. Gibson and to Col. Jacob for their inspiration, guidance, and patience in helping me with this book. I also thank Anna Logan Lawson, an anthropologist and former editor of publications at Hollins College, for her interest in this project and support of its development.

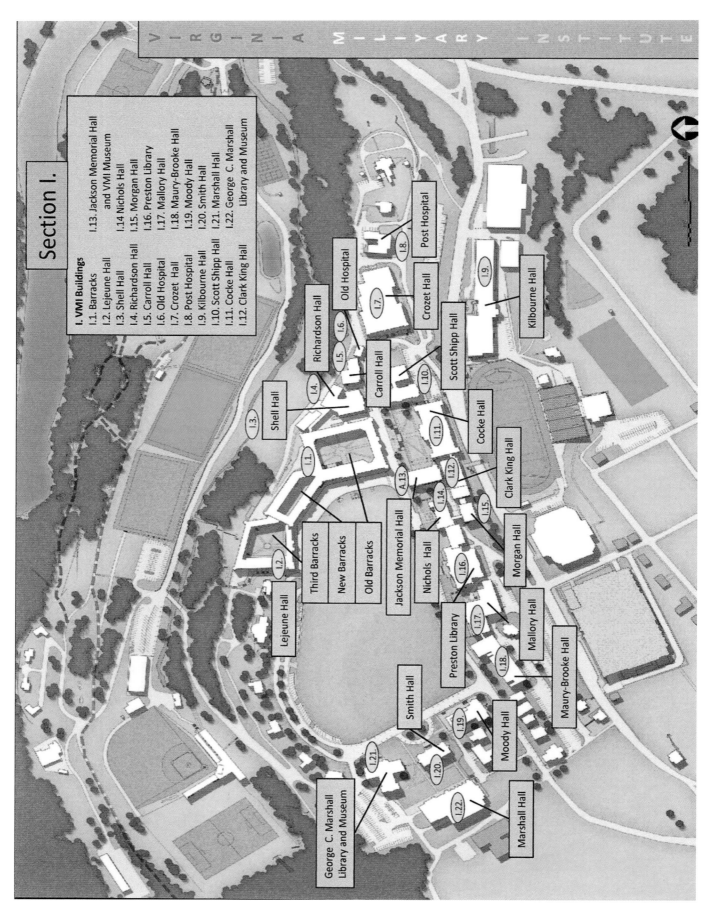

Section I.

I. VMI Buildings
I.1. Barracks
I.2. Lejeune Hall
I.3. Shell Hall
I.4. Richardson Hall
I.5. Carroll Hall
I.6. Old Hospital
I.7. Crozet Hall
I.8. Post Hospital
I.9. Kilbourne Hall
I.10. Scott Shipp Hall
I.11. Cocke Hall
I.12. Clark King Hall
I.13. Jackson Memorial Hall and VMI Museum
I.14 Nichols Hall
I.15. Morgan Hall
I.16. Preston Library
I.17. Mallory Hall
I.18. Maury-Brooke Hall
I.19. Moody Hall
I.20. Smith Hall
I.21. Marshall Hall
I.22. George C. Marshall Library and Museum

VIRGINIA MILITARY INSTITUTE

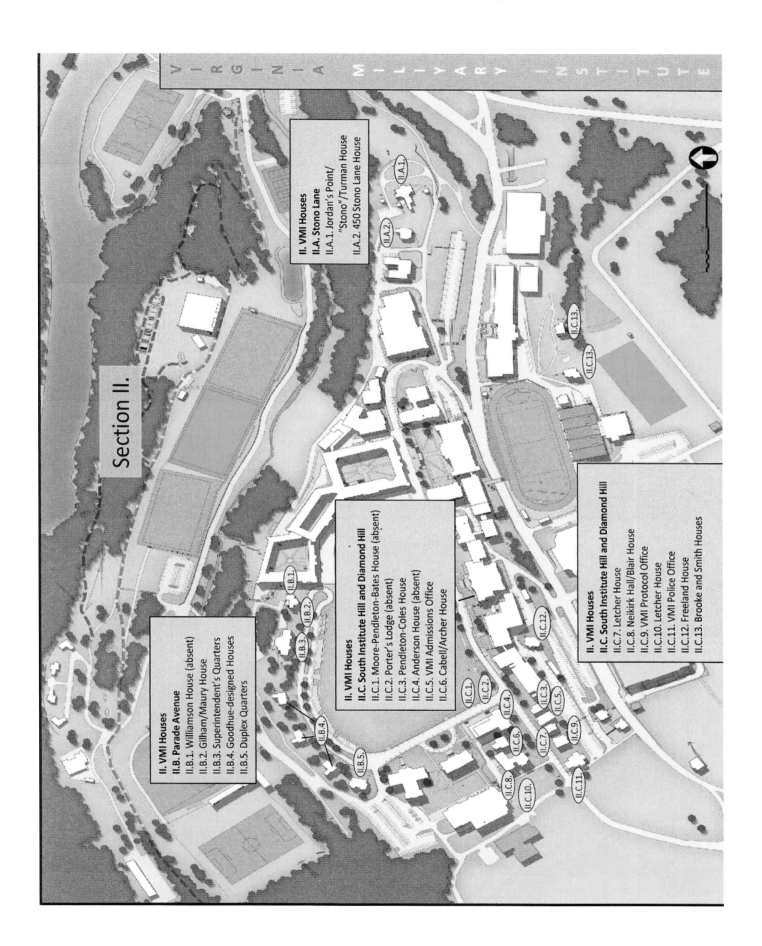

Section II.

II. VMI Houses
II.A. Stono Lane
II.A.1. Jordan's Point/
"Stono"/Turman House
II.A.2. 450 Stono Lane House

II. VMI Houses
II.B. Parade Avenue
II.B.1. Williamson House (absent)
II.B.2. Gilham/Maury House
II.B.3. Superintendent's Quarters
II.B.4. Goodhue-designed Houses
II.B.5. Duplex Quarters

II. VMI Houses
II.C. South Institute Hill and Diamond Hill
II.C.1. Moore-Pendleton-Bates House (absent)
II.C.2. Porter's Lodge (absent)
II.C.3. Pendleton-Coles House
II.C.4. Anderson House (absent)
II.C.5. VMI Admissions Office
II.C.6. Cabell/Archer House

II. VMI Houses
II.C. South Institute Hill and Diamond Hill
II.C.7. Letcher House
II.C.8. Neilkirk Hall/Blair House
II.C.9. VMI Protocol Office
II.C.10. Letcher House
II.C.11. VMI Police Office
II.C.12. Freeland House
II.C.13. Brooke and Smith Houses

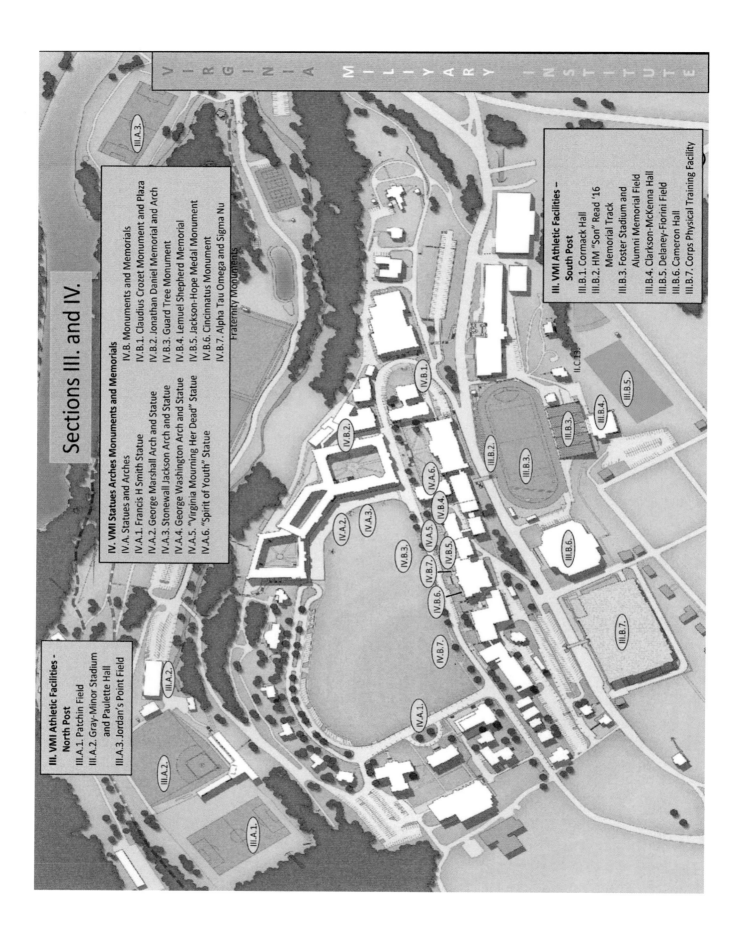

Sections III. and IV.

III. VMI Athletic Facilities - North Post
III.A.1. Patchin Field
III.A.2. Gray-Minor Stadium and Paulette Hall
III.A.3. Jordan's Point Field

IV. VMI Statues Arches Monuments and Memorials

IV.A. Statues and Arches
IV.A.1. Francis H Smith Statue
IV.A.2. George Marshall Arch and Statue
IV.A.3. Stonewall Jackson Arch and Statue
IV.A.4. George Washington Arch and Statue
IV.A.5. "Virginia Mourning Her Dead" Statue
IV.A.6. "Spirit of Youth" Statue

IV.B. Monuments and Memorials
IV.B.1. Claudius Crozet Monument and Plaza
IV.B.2. Jonathan Daniel Memorial and Arch
IV.B.3. Guard Tree Monument
IV.B.4. Lemuel Shepherd Memorial
IV.B.5. Jackson-Hope Medal Monument
IV.B.6. Cincinnatus Monument
IV.B.7. Alpha Tau Omega and Sigma Nu
Fraternity Monuments

III. VMI Athletic Facilities – South Post
III.B.1. Cormack Hall
III.B.2. HM "Son" Read '16
Memorial Track
III.B.3. Foster Stadium and
Alumni Memorial Field
III.B.4. Clarkson-McKenna Hall
III.B.5. Delaney-Fiorini Field
III.B.6. Cameron Hall
III.B.7. Corps Physical Training Facility

Bibliography

Couper, William. *Claudius Crozet*.
The Historical Publishing Company, Inc. Charlottesville, VA. 1936.

Couper, William. *One Hundred Years at V.M. I.*
Garrett and Massie, Inc. Richmond, VA. 1939.

Davis, Thomas W. *A Crowd of Honorable Youths*. Lexington, VA.
VMI Sesquicentennial Committee. 1988.

Davis, Thomas W. *The Corps Roots the Loudest - A History of VMI Athletics*.
University Press of Virginia. Charlottesville, VA. 1986.

Gibson, Keith. *Virginia Military Institute*. Arcadia Publishing. Charleston, SC. 2010

Lyle, Royster and Simpson, Pamela. *The Architecture of Historic Lexington*.
University Press of Virginia. Charlottesville, VA. 1977.

Morgan, James M. *The Jackson-Hope and The Society of the Cincinnati Medals
of the Virginia Military Institute*. McClure Press. Verona, VA. 1979.

Pezzoni, J. Daniel. *The Architecture of Historic Rockbridge*.
Printed in Hong Kong, China. Distributed by University of Virginia Press.   2015

Pogue, Forrest C. *George C. Marshall - Education of a General*.
 W. & G. Baird, LTD. London and Belfast, England. 1964.

Shaffner, Randolph P. *The Father of VMI - A Biography of Colonel J.T.L. Preston, CSA*.
McFarland & Company, Inc. Jefferson, NC. 2014.

Wise, Henry A. *Drawing Out the Man - The VMI Story*.
University Press of Virginia. Charlotteville, VA. 1978.

Section I. VMI Buildings

The buildings at VMI are exquisite, in large part due to the Gothic Revival architectural theme that Alexander Jackson Davis designed. Davis was an architect from New York who was recommended by Phillip St. George Cocke, a member of the VMI Board of Visitors, and supported by Superintendent Francis Smith. The architectural design correlated perfectly with the objective for the Virginia Military Institute to include full military activity as well as college education. When VMI started on 11 November 1839, there were only two buildings – a small barracks that was used by Virginia Militia soldiers and an arsenal building that was used to store rifles and ammunition – and only seven acres of land.

This section of the book will address all buildings at VMI which were named for someone, including those which have been demolished, plus the VMI Barracks. The information will include the locations of the buildings, the dates of construction, the purposes for the buildings, some architectural details, and a brief biography for whom the buildings were named. Pictures of the buildings are included, some of which are very historic and thankfully were provided by the VMI Archives Department and the VMI Museum.

The first building constructed after 1839 was a small mess hall at the location of the present Crozet Hall. A more significant building was Old Barracks which started in 1850. Over the long years, new buildings were added for academics, athletics, Stonewall Jackson Memorial Halls, libraries, museums, administration, and Marshall Hall for conferences, banquets, the annual Ring Figure Ball, and a theater.

I.1. Barracks

The VMI barracks are buildings where cadets sleep, study, receive "Rat Line" discipline, and learn a lot of the VMI character. Barracks are the heart of VMI. When one drives onto the VMI Post, the huge barracks at the east end of the Parade Ground provide a wonderful picture of the Gothic Revival architecture used for VMI. While completely integrated, the barracks consist of three buildings, and the construction timeline may be the longest in United States history, stretching from 1850 to 2008. The "Old Barracks" pictured to the right were started in 1850, but not completed until 1925 due to many difficulties. "New Barracks" is in the middle and was completed in 1949. The last barracks, left in the picture below, was completed in 2008 and called "Third Barracks". The northwest corner of Third Barracks was named Lejuene Hall because the existing Lejuene Hall was demolished to provide property for Third Barracks.

All barracks are four stories tall and the interior includes courtyards and "sallyports" which are openings between the barracks on each floor that allow cadets to walk from one barracks to another. The rooms in the barracks accommodate 3-5 cadets, and have walls all around the room with a window on the outside and a door on the inside. Outside the interior doors are concrete platforms for walking space within barracks. A picture of interior barracks is presented to the right. The barracks include four arched entrances named for George Washington, "Stonewall" Jackson, George Marshall, and Jonathon Daniels.

When the Virginia Military Institute was founded on 11 November 1839, the barracks for 28 cadets and Superintendent Francis H. Smith was built in 1816 for Virginia Militia soldiers assigned to the Virginia Arsenal in Lexington. Consisting of nine rooms, the barracks was only two stories high constructed where now exists the south side of Old Barracks on Letcher Avenue, with a four-story arsenal north of barracks. Unfortunately, the barracks was small and the significant disrepair was described by Smith's comment: "Every conceivable discomfort existed".

In 1843, a Smith developed a plan to extend the barracks. The south side of barracks was comparable to present barracks with adjoining rooms and interior porches called "stoops" running in front of the room doors. The three-story new east wing completed in 1847 had rooms on the inside and outside of the wing, with a hallway in the middle of the wing.

In 1849, a member of the VMI Board of Visitors, Phillip St. George Cocke, recommended that VMI contract with a New York architect, Alexander Jackson Davis, who had designed a Gothic Revival style home in Virginia for Cocke. Fortunately, Davis was hired and he developed a comprehensive architecture plan for VMI, using the Gothic Revival style, which established the present architectural theme for VMI. Davis began work on the plans while Smith, supported by Cocke and other members of the VMI Board of Visitors, attempted to raise necessary construction funds. The Old Barracks design was rectangular, four stories high, and the solitary rooms were planed to house 200 cadets.

The Virginia legislature appropriated $46,000 in March 1850 to begin construction on the proposed barracks and other buildings. Architect Davis immediately completed details for the barracks, sending Smith more drawings, and excavation of the old militia barracks began almost the same day Smith heard the state funds would be forthcoming. John Jordan, by then a member of the VMI Board of Visitors and initial owner of what is now the Turman House, was contracted to do the massive stone work for the barracks foundation, with Smith supervising the construction.

Construction of Old Barracks began on 19 March 1850. The south façade for the new barracks was built approximately 10 feet south of the former Virginia Militia barracks, which were not completely demolished as they were needed for housing until the new barracks were completed. The cornerstone laid at the southwest corner of barracks on 4 July 1850 still exists. A year later, on 8 July 1851, the VMI cadets moved out of the old Virginia Militia barracks into tents at Camp Philip St. George Cocke on what is now the Parade Ground. While in camp, the cadets could see the old barracks being demolished. Because the new barracks were not completed in time to start the academic courses in the fall semester, the cadets marched to Virginia Springs led by a new professor, Major Thomas Jackson. By September 1851, the old militia barracks were demolished, and the south façade of Old Barracks was completed and ready for occupancy.

In March 1852, work began for an area on the east section of barracks, with a small tower overlooking the bluff. By 1859, the west side of barracks had reached the large heavy tower which is next to today's Jackson Arch. Throughout the 1850s, the building of the barracks was continual, and cadets observed the construction. One cadet remembered a great deal of blasting as the foundation for the new sections was being prepared. The larger barracks provided not only more cadet rooms, but also faculty offices, a chemistry laboratory, lecture rooms, debating rooms, and a library. Two additional huge changes occurred in Old Barracks with steam heat instead of wood stoves and gas lights instead of oil lamps.

Old Barracks presented an imposing view from the Valley Road below, now Main Street, with its heavily dressed limestone foundation, its octagonal towers and crenellated parapets. The entrance was named the Washington Arch, and the entire building was covered with stucco, scored to resemble stone. During the next few years, the old arsenal building north of barracks was demolished and construction started on the wing west side of barracks facing the Drill Ground. Extending Old Barracks with the objective of a quadrangle building used a plan of adding 17-foot sections as funds became available. In this picture, the barracks had the complete south wall and two wings on the east and west.

Construction of the planned barracks quadrangle could not be completed as planned, as Confederate guns fired on Fort Sumter in South Carolina on 12 April 1861, and Virginia seceded from the Union on 23 May 1861. At that point, barracks construction was about half completed, but was halted. Worse than the suspended construction was the arrival of Federal troops under Major General David Hunter on 11 June 1864. In retaliation for VMI's participation in the Battle of New Market and the number of VMI graduates in the Confederate Army,

General Hunter's troops did not completely demolish barracks, but historical photographs show the barracks were extremely damaged and the interior of the barracks was completely destroyed by fire. Fortunately, the artillery commander under General Hunter, Henry DuPont, refused Hunter's order to completely destroy barracks. The roof, crenellated parapets, and upper floors partially collapsed, and only a few windows survived the fire.

With no cadet quarters after Hunter's major damage to barracks, the cadets were housed in Richmond for the 1865-66 schoolyear. They returned in 1866 to VMI to live in cabins built between Old Barracks and the Old Hospital where Shell Hall and Carroll Hall now sit. It is

reported that the cadets liked the cabins as they were heated by open coal fires and they were very comfortable in cold weather. Most of the cadets moved back into Old Barracks in December 1866, followed by the cadet officers in February 1867. The steam heating plant was not in the best condition, leaving the barracks' rooms cold. After the cadets left the cabins, they were used for a variety of functions including the surgeon's office, tailor's shop, guard room, and laundry room. The cabins were demolished in 1905 and 1909.

In the 1890s, water could be drawn by cadets for the first time from faucets in the southwest and southeast corners of the Old Barracks courtyard and this started the water supply. Before 1890, water was carried in buckets by cadets from water springs or Woods Creek, which was then called the Nile. There also was a cistern in the barracks courtyard which was fed by rain water from the roof of the building. Running water was introduced in some of the barracks rooms about 1915 and continued with the erection of the north side of Old Barracks in 1923. By 1926, running water was provided to all rooms and, in 1936, each room received hot water.

The picture left was taken in 1887 and shows the Old Barracks rebuilt over 20 years. Although Virginia was in a financial crisis following the Civil War, Smith was able to obtain funds from the faculty, alumni, and citizens of Lexington to rebuild barracks. The picture shows the fire scars remaining from the 1864 burning, and General Smith decided to retain those marks. A. J. Davis, the Institute's original architect, included in his 1861 plans a chapel that would exist over what is now Jackson Arch. He developed more elaborate designs for the chapel in April 1870, but it was not built. In 1883, the VMI Board of Visitors recommended a chapel to be built as a memorial to General Stonewall Jackson. In 1889, the proposal for the Jackson Memorial project was revived, extending Davis' plans by including the Memorial Chapel into the west wing north of Jackson Arch.

General Scott Shipp became the new VMI Superintendent on 1 January 1890. In his first report, Shipp stated his hopes for a Jackson Memorial Hall to be far more than a chapel, including a gymnasium, bathing facilities for the cadets, and large class rooms. In June 1892, several plans were submitted to the VMI Board of Visitors and the plans of architect Isaac Eugene Alexander Rose, a member of the VMI class of 1883, were adopted. Rose's Memorial Hall design deviated considerably from the original symmetrical drawings of the west façade by Davis, and included a new library with the other facilities proposed by Shipp. By June 1893, the foundation was nearly completed, and JM Hall was completed in 1896. The tower section constructed north of Jackson Arch came from Rose's concept, and remains today.

Disregarding Davis' plan for a quadrangular barracks, the first VMI academic building, Smith Hall, was constructed in 1900, approximately where the north side of Old Barracks exists today, and it was named for Superintendent Smith. The picture viewed from inside the barracks courtyard shows the original Jackson Memorial Hall (left) and Smith Hall (right). The Davis plan for Old Barracks and the Gothic

Revival architectural theme had become disregarded with the construction of these buildings.

In 1907, General Edward Nichols became the third VMI Superintendent and, by 1913, he determined that a new architectural plan was needed. National architect Bertram Grosvenor Goodhue was selected by the VMI Board of Visitors to create the new architectural plan, as one of Goodhue's plans was the West Point Chapel. Like Davis, Goodhue embraced the Gothic Revival style of architecture and pursued the quadrangular plan for Old Barracks. As a result, after making a recommendation to the VMI Board of Visitors, the original Jackson Memorial Hall was demolished in 1916 after the present Jackson Memorial Hall was built, and construction of the western side of Old Barracks was restarted. To complete the quadrangular Old Barracks on the north side, the Smith Academic Building was also demolished after a new academic building, Scott Shipp Hall, was completed in 1919. After these decisions, Old Barracks pictured below was completed in 1925 following Davis's original design, plus the turrets and windows in the middle façade designed by Isaac Eugene Alexander Rose.

A campaign started in July 1948 for another major barracks built on a steep slope with an annex on the northwest corner of Old Barracks. The 1907 Library Building was demolished to provide land for building "New Barracks". The construction included a long, narrow basement known as the concourse. In the summer of 1949, the treasurer's office, military store, tailor shop, and other providers of cadets' services moved into the concourse, as well as the alumni and VMI Foundation offices. The bookstore and branch post office were located there also.

The superintendent's office was relocated from Nichols Engineering Hall onto the ground floor of New Barracks to provide Nichols Engineering Hall more space for the electrical and civil engineering departments. The Commandant's office moved from Washington Arch to its present location in Jackson Arch. The ground floor was also occupied by offices of the Dean of the Faculty, military executives, and other offices including some classrooms. Cadets first occupied the New Barracks in September 1949, and there are "sally ports" on each floor that allow cadets to walk easily between New Barracks and Old Barrracks. After the completion of Mallory Hall in 1952 and its rehabilitation in 1955, the major addition to Scott Shipp Hall in 1955, and the new administration building Smith Hall in 1964, cadets were able to occupy all four floors of New Barracks. Space was still provided for officers and battalion rooms on the first floor and the VMI Board of Visitors rooms on the second floor.

When New Barracks was completed, the opening was named Marshall Arch for General George C. Marshall, a VMI alumnus from the Class of 1901. George Marshall was the U.S. Secretary of Defense when he attended the dedication on New Market Day, 15 May 1951.

In order to build "Third Barracks", it was necessary to demolish Lejeune Hall and the northwest corner of Third Barracks was named Lejeune Hall for General Lejeune. The Third Barracks includes 123 cadet rooms and provides cadet services in the area designated as Lejeune Hall. This section includes the VMI Bookstore and the Cadet Commons, a visitors' center and snack bar area.

One of the features of the new Third Barracks was the return of the "Post Clock", which originally hung over Washington Arch in Old Barracks, but was destroyed in 1864 by the General Hunter attack. Also added was the VMI symbol. All of Third Barracks are shown with New Barracks and Old Barracks on the first page of this article.

I.2. Lejeune Hall

There have been two Lejeune Halls at VMI named for General John Archer Lejeune. The first is pictured to the right and was opened in September 1966. It was built on VMI Parade at the same spot as the former Williamson House built in 1852, which was razed in 1965 in order to build Lejeune Hall. The first Lejeune Hall stood to the west of New Barracks, but was demolished in 2006 in order to construct Third Barracks.

The present Lejeune Hall pictured left was built in 2008 and incorporated into the northwestern part of Third Barracks. The first Lejeune Hall had an octagonal exterior, with a two-story three-bay wide arcade facing the Parade Ground. While very useful for the cadets, it had little architectural relationship to the Gothic Revival architectural theme of the VMI Post. However, the building contained numerous cadet services including the Post Exchange, a snack bar, book store, television room, bowling alley and pool tables, reception facilities to meet and entertain guests, and a ballroom for informal dances, conferences, lectures, movies, and art exhibits. The present Lejeune Hall is used to accommodate virtually the same cadet services that were provided in the former Lejeune Hall.

John Archer Lejeune

Lieutenant General John Archer Lejeune was born in Pointe Coupee Parish, Louisiana, on 10 January 1867. He graduated from the U. S. Naval Academy in 1888, went to sea as a Naval Cadet from 1888-1890, and was commissioned a 2nd Lieutenant in the U. S. Marine Corps in 1890. During his distinguished military career, he saw combat duty in both the Spanish-American War and the First World War. Lejeune was promoted to Brigadier General in 1916 and to Major General in 1918, and served as Commandant of the U. S. Marine Corps from 1920-1929, and the Marine base Camp Lejeune in North Carolina was named in his honor.

He served as VMI's fifth Superintendent from 1 July 1929 to 30 September 1937. He arrived when the nation's Great Depression was starting and his friendship with President Roosevelt helped provide needed Federal funding for VMI. In September 1932, Superintendent Lejeune was walking on a steep hillside behind barracks to look at the work in progress on Richardson Hall. He slipped, fell down the hill, and was incapacitated for about a year. He was Superintendent Emeritus until his death on 20 November 1942, at the age of 75, and was honored with a promotion to Lieutenant General before his death. Lejeune wrote of his association with and experience at VMI: "I believe that this school is unexcelled in character-building and in the making of useful, patriotic American citizens."

I.3. Shell Hall

Shell Hall is located on Letcher Avenue, immediately east of Old Barracks, and was named for General George Shell in 2010 after a new science building had been constructed on Letcher Avenue next to the Post Limits Gate and was named Maury-Brooke Hall in 2013. The former name of Shell Hall was Maury-Brooke Hall when it was built in 1909 as the Chemistry Building -- VMI's first building dedicated to the study of science.

The old cabins were demolished to make room for the 1909 chemistry academic building. They were built after the Civil War as quarters for the cadets because Old Barracks had been extremely burned by the Union Army in 1864.

Norfolk architect John Kevan Peebles designed Shell Hall in a Gothic Revival style that closely follows the details established by A. J. Davis for the Old Barracks. Shell Hall is a three-story stuccoed masonry building on a local limestone foundation, with deep crenellated parapets and multi-story diamond-paned windows. The building underwent a major renovation circa 1991 when it was renovated to accommodate its current use for cadet support facilities. Shell Hall is a contributing resource to the VMI Historic District.

Limestone is used for window sills and parapet capstones. Shell Hall has a particularly elaborate crenellated roof line, which is patterned after the Old Barracks parapets. The main south façade is five-bays wide with a slight projection at the center three-bays. The main central entrance has an elaborate crenellated entrance with a basket-handle arched doorway. The double entrance doors are modern plain wood doors with brass hardware. Windows at the main elevation are diamond-paned wood casement sash with diamond-paned transoms. Lintels are decorated with a low-relief keystone. The windows are placed singly as well as in groups of four set in three-story panels. Vertical board wood panels span the areas between floor levels. At all other facades, the windows are plain double hung, one-over-one windows with a pivot sash transom.

The interior of Shell Hall was refinished with modern materials during a 1991 renovation project. However, the original stairwell and railings were retained at the south central stair. The newel post at the staircase has Gothic Revival detailing. All other spaces have modern finishes.

George Richard Edwin Shell

Lieutenant General George Richard Edwin Shell was born on 20 October 1908 in Hampton, Virginia, and died on 30 October 1996, at the age of 88, in Baltimore, Maryland. He graduated from VMI in the Class of 1931 with a Bachelor's Degree in Electrical Engineering. As a cadet, George R. E. Shell served as vice president of his class, member of the Honor Court, a lieutenant in the Corps, and was a varsity letterman in both football and wrestling.

His distinguished career as a U. S. Marine Corps officer began with his commissioning in 1931. During World War II, he commanded an artillery battalion in the Pacific Theater and was awarded the Purple Heart and Legion of Merit with a combat "V" device which distinguishes an award for heroism or valor in combat. He subsequently served in many assignments throughout his 29 years of active duty including on the staff of the Joint Chiefs of Staff at the Pentagon; the staff of SHAPE (*Supreme Headquarters Allied Powers Europe)*, which is headquarters for NATO (North Atlantic Treaty Organization) in Mons, Belgium; and commanding general at the Marine Recruit Depot, Parris Island, South Carolina.

He became VMI's ninth Superintendent on 1 July 1960, serving until 30 June 1971. Under his leadership, VMI saw extensive academic, military, and facilities revitalization. New construction under his tenure at VMI included Smith Hall, Lejeune Hall, Kilbourne Hall, Moody Hall, Alumni Memorial Stadium, Marshall Library, annexes to Nichols Engineering and Cocke Hall, and the Hall of Valor at New Market Battlefield State Historical Park. Following his retirement, he faithfully served the Lexington community for more than 20 years. He was also on the VMI Alumni Association Board from 31 December 1979 to 31 December 1981. After he died in Baltimore, Maryland, he was buried in the Stonewall Jackson Memorial Cemetery in Lexington, Virginia.

I.4. Richardson Hall

Richardson Hall is connected northeast to Shell Hall along the ridge overlooking Woods Creek. It was named for William Harvie Richardson who had a number of positions with the State of Virginia and was a large supporter of VMI.

Originally designed for chemistry labs, Richardson Hall was completed in 1935 behind and as an adjunct to the Chemistry Building then named Maury-Brooke Hall, which is now Shell Hall. It is a utilitarian building that has served many needs of the VMI Post, first as a chemistry laboratory and, in 1997, was converted to a military store and tailor shop. Its location did not require elaborate architectural detailing, however, its overall appearance was designed to blend in with the surrounding Gothic Revival architecture.

Before the construction of Richardson Hall, an old building at that site was demolished in 1934. The old building (pictured to the right) was constructed in 1851 for use as a power house to provide heat for the barracks rooms. The old building was later used as a laundry and as a temporary mess hall after the Civil War because the mess hall had been burned by the Union Army. It was also used as the arsenal for VMI cadets after 1869, and the weapons were moved to the sub-basement of Cocke Hall in 1933. In 1893, the old building became known as the Chemistry Building and VMI manufactured its own gas from coal for use in the laboratories. A new chemistry building was constructed in 1909, and is now named Shell Hall.

Richardson Hall is a masonry structure clad with stucco and cast stone trim. The two-story, rectangular building measures three-bays deep and seven-bays long and has a full basement built into the slope of the hill. The flat roof has crenellated parapet walls. It is linked to the north façade of Shell Hall with a three-bay wide, two-story connecting structure. A tunnel runs through this connector at ground level for pedestrian access. Windows are multi-paned with fixed metal sashes. The basement level has large louver panels. The main entrance is located on the southwest façade, and is fitted with a modern, glazed metal door. The interior is utilitarian and has been upgraded with new systems and finishes.

An elevated concrete walkway provides a direct connection between Old Barracks an the cadet service support areas found within Richardson and Shell Halls (i.e., military store, tailor, laundry, post office). Richardson Hall is a contributing resource to the VMI Historic District.

William Harvie Richardson

Richardson was born in Richmond, Virginia on 18 December 1795. His life was fully committed to service for the State of Virginia. He began at the age of seventeen in the Virginia Militia in the War of 1812, and served later as the Virginia's first State Librarian, Secretary of the Commonwealth, and Adjutant General from 1841 to 1876, except for 1865 to 1870 after the Civil War. He was also the longest member of the VMI Board of Visitors from 1841 to 1876. However, he was an ex-officio member in 1865 and 1866, when the new Governor Pierpoint took over the Virginia government after the Civil War and removed Richardson from the board in May 1865.

A portrait of Richardson (not the picture to the right) was painted by the artist William Hubard, who was also the sculptor of the George Washington statue. Portraits of General Braxton and Colonel Smith were formally presented to the Institute by Philip St. George Cocke during the finals of 1853, at which time the Society of Alumni made arrangements to add another, that of General Richardson.

On 30 May 1837, Richardson was Secretary of the Virginia Commonwealth and sent a notice to the Virginia Adjutant General informing him of the four men appointed by Governor David Campbell to the first VMI Board of Visitors. Claudius Crozet was elected president of the board. On 11 July 1839, Richardson signed an Executive Order by order of the governor which was inserted in multiple newspapers in Virginia notifying people that VMI would begin on 11 November 1839.

As the first Virginia Librarian, Richardson engaged in the collection of books for about 12 years. On the last day of 1839, he submitted a report to the General Assembly recommending that duplicate books in the Virginia state library be transferred to VMI for the establishment of its library. The General Assembly agreed and passed a joint resolution that led to the founding of the VMI library. His interest in the VMI library continued for many years and the first books were shipped in September 1840. With the shipment, he included an application for the admission of his only son. Additional aid came from the legislature appropriating $500 a year for five years to build the VMI library.

In 1841, General Richardson proposed to VMI Superintendent Colonel Smith that a third professor be added to the VMI faculty. As a result, Thomas Williamson of Norfolk, a classmate and roommate of Colonel Smith for four years at West Point, was hired and guided the engineering instruction at VMI for 47 years.

Unrelated to VMI, Richardson became the proprietor and occupant of a farm in 1841, and prepared a plan for the organization of an agricultural and horticultural society. This led to the Virginia Agricultural Society, for which Philip St. George Cocke was an enthusiastic number and served as president of the society.

On 20 November 1841, Colonel Smith requested that Richardson procure a flag for VMI, which he did. And, in December 1841, Richardson was the Virginia Adjutant General and sent a letter to the VMI Superintendent Colonel Smith with an order from the governor to bring officers and cadets from VMI to meet with the General Assembly in order to give the legislators a good idea of the institution they had founded. Richardson was the person who prepared and presented that order to the governor. It was reported by Claudius Crozet that the cadets made a favorable impression to the legislature in January 1842, and a legislature act was passed in March 1842 increasing funds for VMI by $1500.

Before the first VMI commencement in 1842, Colonel Smith sent a letter to Richardson requesting that the governor sign 16 of the diplomas that would be sent to him from New York. The VMI diplomas have always been signed by the governor of Virginia and this makes it necessary to send them to Richmond. In the early days, Richardson made it a part of his duty to take the diplomas to Lexington. His letter of 29 June 1842 reads: "I shall go on the packet boat tomorrow morning to Lynchburg and will probably not reach Lexington until Monday. I shall bring the diplomas with me". Smith also requested that Richardson purchase 16 small pocket Bibles inscribed in gold with the name of the VMI graduates which were presented on 4 July 1842. The diplomas presented to VMI graduates today are approximately the same as the first.

In 1848, Superintendent Smith made a recommendation to the VMI Board of Visitors to request $50,000 from the Virginia legislature to remove the old Virginia militia barracks and construct a new building. A number of members on the VMI Board of Visitors regarded the application as unwise but it was strongly supported by Board members General Richardson and Philip St. George Cocke, who had obtained the architect A.J. Davis. It was noted that Richardson was the most emphatic in his opinion that the General Assembly would appropriate the necessary means. Richardson also provided the thought that better results might be obtained in presenting the case to the legislature if a construction plan was provided also. As a result, when Major Gilham went to New York to purchase equipment for VMI he met with A.J. Davis discussing the architecture needed for VMI. While it has been reported that Philip Cocke was the person who recommended AJ Davis (because Davis was the architect for his house called Belmeade, which had a Gothic revival theme), Richardson also recommended to Gilham before meeting A.J. Davis that the Gothic revival architectural theme be used for VMI buildings.

When an act was passed by the Virginia legislation in 1849 with strong consideration for moving VMI to another location, Richardson, a strong supporter of VMI, stated he was strongly impressed with the necessity of removing VMI to a place out of the way of local jealousies in Lexington and where VMI will have suitable ground for the exercises of cavalry and horse artillery. Three days before the general assembly passed the act requiring the VMI Board of Visitors to investigate other locations for VMI, Superintendent Smith sent an interesting letter to Richardson that Mount Vernon might be the appropriate new location. Smith stated that erecting the Washington Monument at Mount Vernon would transmit his virtues to prosperity and moving VMI to Mount Vernon would make Virginia's sons the bodyguards.

Following the VMI construction plan, there were unexpected obstacles including a number of local citizens in Lexington voiced objections to the location of the military school in their community, and rivalry had developed also between the VMI and neighboring Washington College. Smith felt there was an unfriendly, if not hostile, attitude by some Lexington citizens toward VMI, and felt that the trustees and faculty of Washington College had seriously attempted to restrict the progress of the Institute. During the controversy, there arose another deterrent to the building program. The Virginia General Assembly, taking into consideration the local problems felt by Smith and the limited hilltop setting of the Post, directed that other towns in Virginia, including Winchester and Alexandria, should be considered as potential sites for VMI.

At that point, the Lexington community took a strong look at VMI in a public meeting in which former Virginia Governor James McDowell of Lexington presided. After considerable discussion, the citizens passed a resolution urging retention of VMI in Lexington and called on Washinton College to join in a similar resolution. Within a month, the trustees of Washington College resolved that they had no desire to remove the Virginia Military Institute, while emphacizing the goal to pursue a harmonious relationship between the two institutions. It is presumable that Washington College supported VMI due to John T.L. Preston who was a graduate of Washington College, the "Father of VMI", and an initial faculty member for VMI. After Lexington citizens and Washington & Lee provided support for retaining VMI in Lexington, there was no effort by the general assembly to remove VMI. The matter of local support having been resolved, following a year-long struggle, the Virginia legislature appropriated $46,000 in March 1850 to begin construction on the proposed barracks and other buildings.

On 1 September 1852, the cadets moved into the newly built barracks. By the end of the month, a supply of 300 muskets which had been manufactured by order of the President of the United States was issued to the cadets at VMI. They were the same muskets as those used by the cadets at West Point. According to the report of the VMI Board of Visitors, the muskets received by VMI were due to efforts by Richardson.

In 1855, the Society of the Alumni, now the Alumni Association, presented VMI with a portrait of Richardson. As a strong supporter of VMI, Richardson obtained an invitation for the VMI cadets to attend dedication of the George Washington statue on 26 January 1858 in Richmond Virginia. There were 142 cadets under the command of Commandant Major Gilham. The trip was made by canal to Lynchburg and then by railroad to Richmond, and the cadets received lots of praise and accolades.

There are numerous examples of the very strong connection between Richardson and Superintendent Smith during the Civil War. For example, Richardson rescued two 24 pounder cannons, and they arrived at VMI on 8 June 1863 on the canal boat Fawn. They now sit on both sides of the Washington statue across from Old Barracks. And, in 1874, Richardson was responsible for obtaining from the Washington Armory the guns of the old cadet battery which now sit in front of the Stonewall Jackson statue. In August 1863, Richardson prepared a letter which he and Smith sent to the governor requesting that two rifles and 200 rounds of ammunition for each rifle be sent immediately to VMI for each cadet. As a result, 200 Austrian rifles were sent to VMI with other materials on 11 November 1863. Letters from Richardson report on cadets immediately being sent to Richmond after the Battle at New Market, and fighting to defend Richmond in the Fall of 1864 and providing service at Fort Lee. When the cadets arrived in Richmond, the Confederate House of Representatives passed a resolution on 23 May 1864 unanimously complementing the cadets for their gallant conduct in the Battle of New Market. Clearly, Richardson wanted to protect the cadets. One of the things Richardson did consistently while on the VMI Board of Visitors was to push hard to reduce what he termed as "mistreating new cadets".

In April 1866, an editorial appeared in the Lexington paper praising Richardson. It read "it affords us sincere pleasure to announce to our readers, that General William H. Richardson, the true gentleman, the sterling patriot, the faithful, honest, and efficient officer, has been appointed adjutant general of Virginia. No man in the state is so well qualified for the position on the score of ability, experience and familiarity with the duties. No man possesses in a higher degree the virtues of integrity, impartiality and industry. He never surrenders principle to policy, never comprises, but always trudges the path of duty with a firm and steady step."

On 10 July 1868, Richardson advised the Superintendent Smith that General Grant and General Schofield had advised Richardson that the Ordnance Department cannot issue arms to the VMI cadets, but they could be purchased. Almost immediately, three VMI alumni donated funds to the Corps of Cadets providing them with muskets and swords.

The absence of General Richardson at VMI Finals in 1876 foreshadowed his death on 1 September 1876. Since 1841, he had been present at every annual meeting of the Board of Visitors, except in 1869, when he was temporarily out of office, and in 1874, when his old age and infirmities compelled him to be absent. He left the VMI Board of Visitors meeting at the Exchange Hotel in Richmond on 18 January 1875, when his last appearance with the board was recorded. That day he had voted with the others to grant diplomas to all members of the New Market Corps.

When William Harvie Richardson died on 1 September 1876, at age 81, he left half of his estate to the Virginia Military Institute. His connection with VMI was unique in many ways, and no one has served for a longer period as a member of the VMI Board of Visitors. He was buried in Richmond at the Hollywood Cemetery.

I.5. Carroll Hall

Carroll Hall is located to the east of Old Barracks, west of Letcher Avenue, sited between Shell Hall and The Old Hospital. In 1980, it was named for "Doc" Carroll, a VMI faculty member for 40 years. Constructed in 1904, Carroll Hall was designed by Lynchburg architects Edward Graham Frye and Aubrey Chesterman in the Gothic Revival style of VMI. The diamond-paned windows and crenellated roof line mimic

those in the Old Barracks. This Gothic Revival-style stuccoed masonry building was initially two stories tall and featured crenellated parapet walls, a central square tower, and an octagonal turret. It was originally known as the Administration Building, which also housed a cafe, the tailor shop and the Treasurer's Office.

In 1934, the building was converted to the Biology Academic building and a third floor addition was added that included faculty apartments, including one for Herb Patchin. A major renovation was undertaken circa 1990 in order to convert the academic building into its current use for administrative and academic support facilities, when a new academic building now named Maury-Brooke Hall was constructed in 1988 and provided space for the Biology Department. Carroll Hall is a contributing resource to the VMI Historic District.

Robert Patrick "Doc" Carroll

"Doc" Carroll was born in Alvin, Texas, on 27 May 1903, and moved with his family to Winfall, Virginia, south of Lynchburg, a month later. He earned a Bachelor of Science and Master's degree in Biology at the University of Virginia. He taught for two years in the Biology Department at Washington and Lee University before joining the VMI Chemistry Department in 1928. Colonel Carroll was the first, and for 19 years, VMI's only full-time instructor in the pre-med chemistry course which became a degree-granting program in 1933. After the Biology Department was created in 1933, "Doc" was appointed head of the Department. Carroll taught at VMI for 40 years, retiring in

1968, with 32 years as head of the Biology Department as he stepped down in 1965.

"Doc" Carroll was honored in many ways. The Robert P. Carroll Educational Fund was established in 1967 within the VMI Foundation. Income from the fund is used for the benefit of the Biology Department and selected biology majors. During his years at VMI, Colonel Carroll was also active in civic service working with the Boy Scouts, the Christmas Basket Program, the Virginia Cancer Society, and the Virginia Tuberculosis Association.

A well-known Virginia naturalist, Colonel Carroll worked with the State Forest Service in conservation, fish and game projects, and the James River Study Commission. He was also editor of the Virginia Archeological Society quarterly magazine and became a Fellow of the Virginia Academy of Science in 1972. Upon retirement, Colonel Carroll lived in Millboro, Virginia, Nacogdoches, Texas, Beaufort, South Carolina, and Mars Hill, North Carolina where he died on 18 April 1994, at the age of 90. He was buried in the Stonewall Jackson Memorial Cemetery in Lexington, Virginia.

I.6. Old Hospital

Located east of Old Barracks, the Old Hospital is on the north side of Letcher Avenue between Carroll Hall and Crozet Hall. Constructed in 1849 as a hospital, the Old Hospital is the oldest remaining building on the VMI Post other than the Stono/Turman House which was built in 1818. The Old Hospital served as the VMI hospital until 1870, when the Samuel Jordan residence on Stono Lane behind Crozet Hall was

used for medical services and was officially named the Post Hospital in 1909. After 1870, the Old Hospital had various functions and, today, it serves as an administrative building, providing offices for International Programs and the Institute Chaplain. The Old Hospital is listed as a contributing historical building to the VMI Historic District, and is significant in VMI history.

The Old Hospital is a vernacular-painted brick structure that predates the Gothic Revival era at VMI, and was built on a local limestone foundation. The main southwest façade is three-bays wide with a central entrance at both the first and second floors. The rear, northeast façade is three-bays wide with modern, fixed-sash wood windows and doors at the basement level. The southeast facade has no openings. Window panes are six-over-six in double-hung wood sashes. The doorways have single, glazed wood doors. The interior end-chimneys stand at the northwest and southeast facades.

The second-story porch extends across the main southwest façade. The wood porch is supported by brick piers at the first story and square wood columns at the second story. The porch has a shed-style, standing seam metal roof. Multi-story porches that covered an entire façade were typical for both vernacular and high-style buildings in the South during the mid-to-late-nineteenth century. The two-story porch would have provided shade and protection for hospital patients.

The interior of the Old Hospital retains the overall double-pile, central hall plan. The office spaces have been renovated with modern finishes. Some historical finishes remain, though it is not clear that they date to the original construction. For example, the central stairwell may retain the original wood stairs and railings, and the decorative newel post resembles the newel post at Superintendent Smith's retirement home at 503 Brooke Lane, which dates to 1885.

I.7. Crozet Hall

Crozet Hall is located on the elliptical curve of Letcher Avenue east of Scott Shipp Hall, and the buildings here have always been called the "mess hall". Crozet Hall was built in 1934 and named for the first VMI Board of Visitor's  president, Claudius Crozet. It was built on the same site of four earlier mess hall buildings constructed first in 1840, in 1854 when designed by A.J. West, in 1866 built again on the Davis plan after the 1854 building was burned in 1864 by the Union Army, and 1905 after the mess hall was again burned in 1904. The 1905 mess hall was demolished in 1934 to in order to construct Crozet Hall in 1935. Crozet Hall was designed in the VMI Gothic Revival style to harmonize with the existing VMI Post environment, with stuccoed masonry, a cross-gabled roof and a central sally-port flanked by square turrets. It is a contributing resource to the VMI Historic District.

Crozet Hall has served as a mess hall for VMI cadets since its original construction. A major expansion and renovation of Crozet Hall increasing the mess hall capacity began in 2004, completed in 2006, and required the demolition of a 1903 Queen Anne residence on Stono Lane behind Crozet Hall. It had served as the Post Surgeon's residence, and was one of a matched pair designed by Lexington architect William G. McDowell built on both sides of the Post Hospital.

fore the two-story wooden mess hall was built in 1840, food for cadets and faculty was pared in the southeast wing of the original Virginia Arsenal barracks, and served in the nal building. A kitchen, the dining room and the steward's quarters were on the ground and the upstairs floor included section rooms for Engineering and French classes, as well oom for meetings such as the Society of Cadets. "Hops" were held in the mess hall with g on the first floor and dinner on the second floor. By the end of 1840, a third floor was ted for lecture rooms. One of the rooms on the third floor was used as a library.

The original mess hall was demolished in 1854 in order to build a new mess hall funded by Virginia and designed by A. J. Davis in the Gothic Revival style. Completed in 1854, it was a symmetrical two-and-one-half story stuccoed brick building, and the main entrance had a wide sally-port flanked by crenellated square towers. In addition to the dining room, quarters were made for the VMI Board of Visitors, the steward's family, and various officers. Rooms were also provided for the cooks, waiters and kitchen helpers. Unfortunately, it was burned out by General Hunter in 1864, but it was rebuilt to Davis' plan in 1865-1866.

Regrettably, the mess hall was burned out again in 1904, and rebuilt on its original foundation in 1905. Designed by Lynchburg architects Edward Graham Frye and Aubrey Chesterman, the 1905 Mess Hall was a scaled-down version of the 1854 Davis building. It was a full story shorter than its predecessor at one-and-one-half stories. Like its predecessor, it was a stuccoed masonry building with a cross-gabled roof and central sally-port flanked by square turrets. This mess hall was later demolished in 1934 to make room for the present Crozet Hall in 1935. Greatly increasing the mess hall capacity, Crozet Hall is a long two-story building with a central bay marked by the pair of engaged octagonal turrets.

A major expansion and renovation of Crozet Hall increasing the mess hall capacity was completed in 2006, constructed against the east façade of the original mess hall. It remains a masonry structure supported on a local limestone foundation and clad in painted stucco with cast stone trim. The two-story building is rectangular in plan and now measures 13-bays long and seven bays deep. The flat roof has crenellated parapet walls and drains to internal downspouts. The north, south, and central bays project slightly, and each has its own entrance. The central bay has a triangular parapet wall with flanking, wide octagonal turrets. Decorative buttresses stand between each window bay, and the windows over the entrance doors are triple sashes. The entrance doors are double, glazed wood doors with a basket-handle arch. The brick paving in front of Crozet Hall is notable with Lexington bricks used to define the entry.

Related to the mess hall is an interesting history about the original water and ice at VMI. Initially, cadets had to carry water in buckets from springs or Woods Creek, which was also called "the Nile". Fortunately, a project was completed which provided water for the Institute from the waterworks of the town of Lexington. It was a simple water system, with only a few faucets and a small main, but a vast improvement over the method of hauling water from the springs. The waterline terminated at first in a fountain in front of the mess hall, but a year later the pipes were conducted to the kitchen, thus, adding greatly to the convenience and safety of the operations. Water was also provided by a cistern which was fed by rainwater from the roof of the building.

In the 1890s, water could be drawn by the cadets from faucets installed in the corners of the southwest and southeast corners of the Old Barracks courtyard on each stoop. This was the only source of water supply for about 20 years. Running water was introduced into some of the rooms about 1915, and installation continued with construction of the north side of Old

Barracks in 1923. By 1926, running water was conducted to all rooms and, in 1936, each room was also served with hot water.

Related to the water history, construction of an icehouse was located on the Parade Ground in a sinkhole where the Superintendent's Quarters were built in 1860. As a result of that residence construction, the icehouse was moved to a fork in the road near the southwest corner of the mess hall, and was a building well known to several generations of cadets. Each winter, a supply of ice was cut from the nearby waterways in sufficient quantities for use over the summer months. At first, a pond formed by a dam across Woods Creek, approximately and rear of the hospital, was a source of supply, but the ice was later obtained from the North River, which is now Maury River. The icehouse was no longer needed in 1916 and was razed.

Claudius Crozet

Crozet was born in Villefranche, France on 31 December 1789. He was educated at the L'École Polytechnique in Paris, and served in the Napoleonic Wars as a captain in the artillery under Napoleon Bonaparte. He became a prisoner in Russia for two years following the Moscow campaign and the defeat of Napoleon in the Battle of Leipzig in October 1813. After he was released, Crozet traveled to the United States in 1816 and, with a recommendation from Marquis de Lafayette, became assistant professor of engineering at the United States Military Academy (West Point), a position he held from 1817 to 1823.

In 1823, the Virginia Board of Public Works elected Crozet as Virginia's Principal Engineer and Surveyor, and Crozet departed for Richmond, ending his duties at West Point. Crozet was actively engaged in hundreds of public improvement projects for Virginia, including the building of canals, roads, and railroads. Perhaps most importantly, he directed the building of the first railroad tunnels through Virginia's Blue Ridge Mountains as early as 1839. The Blue Ridge Railroad was incorporated by the Commonwealth of Virginia in 1849 with Claudius Crozet as chief engineer. Its plan was to provide a crossing of the Blue Ridge Mountains for the Virginia Central Railroad into the Shenandoah Valley.

Overseen by Crozet, the crossing was accomplished by building four tunnels, including the 4,273-foot Blue Ridge Tunnel near the top of Afton Mountain. With construction proceeding from either side, a decade before the invention of dynamite, the complex was dug though solid granite with only hand drills and black powder. The tunnel was less than 6 inches off perfect alignment when it was holed through on 29 December 1856. When completed, the Blue Ridge

Tunnel was the longest in the United States. It opened to rail traffic in April 1858, and was considered to be one of the engineering wonders of the modern world.

As a graduate of the L'École Polytechnique and an artillery officer, Crozet also gained extensive experience as an educator at West Point, so when the time came to set up military culture at VMI, he was appointed by the Virginia Governor as first president of the VMI Board of Visitors on 1 July 1937, and he continued as president until 1845, and remained on the Board until 1 July 1848. He is also credited with major contributions to VMI's academic program and military organization.

Crozet was principal of the Richmond Academy from 1859 to his death on 29 January 1864. Originally buried in Shockoe Hill Cemetery in Richmond, he was reinterred on the grounds of the Virginia Military Institute located in the front of Preston Library in 1942, and moved to the Crozet Plaza area in 2007, across the street from Crozet Hall on Letcher Avenue.

The Plaza is described in this book at Section IV.B.1.

I.8. Post Hospital

The Post Hospital is located behind Crozet Hall on Stono Lane. It was originally a Greek Revival residence constructed in 1850 by John Jordan for his son Samuel Jordan. VMI purchased the house in 1870 for medical services and the Old Hospital stopped serving that function. However, the Jordan house was not named the Post Hospital until 1909. The original Jordan residence has been altered both inside and out, and the building has provided medical service to VMI staff, faculty, and cadets until today. It is now a part of the VMI Historic District.

The original 1850 residence was a two-story, five-bay wide, two-bay deep brick structure. The front is still dominated by a two-story porch, which extends across the south facade and wraps around the southeast and southwest corners. The porch is supported by square wood columns. The windows are six-over-six, double-hung wood sash fitted with exterior screens. There are two main entrances at the first and second floor levels on the south façade. Each entrance has a single-glazed wood door with flanking three-light sidelights. Secondary entrances are located behind the building on the north and northwest façades. The interior has been completely rehabilitated for hospital services and healthcare facilities, eliminating internal historical finishes.

In 1909, the historical five-bay main façade was expanded with two wing additions. The northeast wing is two stories tall, six bays long, and two bays wide. The hipped roof is covered with standing seam metal, and the windows are paired, including steel casement sash and fixed transom lights above. The northwest wing has similar proportions to the northeast wing. On the south façade, the northwest wing has a two-story, glassed-in porch that copies the original 1850 porch details. The northwest wing is brick, with a one-story addition at the north end. Windows in the northwest wing are six-over-six, double-hung wood sash fitted with exterior screens.

I.9. Kilbourne Hall

Kilbourne Hall is located south of Main Street, between Alumni Memorial Field and the Cormack Field House. Presently used for all Reserve Officer Training Corps (ROTC) departments, this building has a long history going back to 1919. The building to the right of the white main entrance was named for Lieutenant General Charles Kilbourne in 1968, and Kilbourne Hall now is essentially an assemblage of two buildings joined together in 2009 with the white-faced centerpiece.

The building left of the white centerpiece was initially used as horse stables. On 7 July 1919, one hundred horses arrived at the Institute and were put out to pasture. By fall, the stables were ready. Of the hundred horses assigned to VMI, 40 were sent to the field artillery branch to pull VMI's howitzers and the remaining 60 went to the cavalry branch. Forty enlisted U. S. Army soldiers assigned to VMI to care for the animals and equipment. These soldiers served as blacksmiths, groomers, and stable hands.

The original stables, made of wood, were torn down in 1939, and replaced by a more modern steel and masonry structure. The Institute's horse population grew to 160 horses by 1939, and 180 by 1945. VMI's school colors are based on the old red, white, and yellow branch colors carried by the field artillery, infantry, and cavalry during this period. The decision after WWII to eliminate the Army cavalry effectively ended the horse association with VMI. Horses made their last appearance during the final garrison review in June 1948, ending VMI's affiliation with horses. On 6 April 1949, the old stables were rededicated as the new ROTC facility complete with classrooms, offices, and storage areas, and renovated with state funds.

The original Kilbourne Hall, the building to the right of the white centerpiece, was completed in 1968 and provided new classrooms for ROTC training. At that time, the former stables and ROTC classrooms became offices for the Buildings and Grounds Department, later named the VMI Physical Plant. In 1974, more ROTC space was needed with the continued enlargement of the Corps and the addition of Navy/Marine Corps ROTC. Thus, the VMI Physical Plant was moved and the former stables building underwent rehabilitation to create more ROTC space. In 2009, a new main entrance was constructed to join the 1939 and 1968 structures, creating a new and larger Kilbourne Hall – probably the largest ROTC building in the nation.

Charles Evan Kilbourne

General Kilbourne was born at Fort Meyer, Virginia, on 23 December 1872. He was a VMI graduate in the Class of 1894, receiving the Jackson-Hope Medal, Second Honor. His Brother Rat William Horner Cocke, received the Jackson-Hope Medal, First Honor. Kilbourne served for 38 years in the U.S. Army.

He entered the volunteer Signal Corps as a 2nd Lieutenant at the outbreak of the Spanish-American War in 1898, and received the Medal of Honor for gallantry in action in the Philippines in 1899. He received his regular Army commission in 1899, and served in China during the Boxer Rebellion.

During World War I, he was Chief of Staff of the 89th Division and was wounded in action in France. He was promoted to Brigadier General in 1928, and was assigned to the War Department's War Plans Division. He received his promotion to Major General in 1935 and retired the next year. He was the first person in American history to hold simultaneously the nation's three highest military awards: the Medal of Honor, the Distinguished Service Cross, and the Distinguished Service Medal.

After serving in the United States Army from 1898 to 1936, General Kilbourne was selected as VMI's sixth Superintendent, serving from 1 October 1937 until he retired on 20 June 1946. While he was the VMI Superintendent, there were multiple events including the VMI Centennial Celebration in 1939 and the transfer of the remains of Claudius Crozet in 1942 from Shockoe Cemetery in Richmond, Virginia, to a grave near the entrance to Preston Library. He also guided the Institute through the challenging years of World War II. On 7 December 1941, the day Pearl Harbor in Hawaii was attacked by Japan, General Kilbourne called the Corps of Cadets into Jackson Memorial Hall and admonished them not to enlist in the Army, but to remain at VMI and complete their education. Within 24 months, however, many cadets including James M. Morgan, Jr. saw their education interrupted and left for active duty service. General Kilbourne died on 12 November 1963 at the age of 90, and was buried in the National Arlington Cemetery.

I.10. SCOTT SHIPP HALL

Scott Shipp Hall is located on Letcher Avenue southeast of Old Barracks, and east and adjacent to Memorial Garden and Cocke Hall. It was named for Scott Shipp who was a VMI graduate and the second superintendent at VMI. It was designed by the architectural firm of Carneal and Johnston, and completed in 1919, consistent with the VMI Gothic Revival architectural theme. It housed many of the offices and classrooms formerly housed in the former Smith Academic

Building. With the completion of Scott Shipp Hall, the Smith Academic Building was demolished in order to allow the north section of Old Barracks to be built.

A major addition was added to the east of Scott Shipp Hall in 1955. The addition was a five-story rectangular building constructed perpendicular to the original building. It is linked to the east façade of the main building with an adjoining, four-story connector. Both the addition and the original building underwent interior renovations in 1994. Scott Shipp Hall has served as the Liberal Arts Building from its initial construction to the present, and is a contributing resource to the VMI Historic District.

CHARLES ROBERT SCOTT SHIPP

Scott Ship was born 2 August 1839, in Warrenton, Virginia, the year VMI was founded. He dropped the names Charles Robert in 1883, and replaced them with his mother's maiden name Scott, who died in 1879, and he added one "p" to his last name for Shipp.

Upon graduation from VMI in 1859, he joined the faculty and served as professor of Latin, mathematics and other subjects at VMI for 29 years. Early in the Civil War, Shipp held the rank of Major in the 21st Infantry (CSA). From 1862 to 1889 he was Commandant of Cadets and commanded the victorious VMI Corps of Cadets at the Battle of New Market on 15 May 1864. At Washington & Lee University next to VMI, he earned the Doctor of Letters in 1883, the year he changed his name, and earned the Doctor of Law in 1890.

In the meetings held by the Board of Visitors on 12 and 13 August 1880 at the Virginia Agricultural and Mechanical College (now Virginia Tech) founded in 1872 in Blacksburg, Virginia, VMI's Colonel Shipp was elected the college president. It is reported that Colonel Shipp was very disappointed with the Board of Visitors, resigned his presidency after only four days, and returned to VMI.

Shipp was appointed Superintendent in 1890 and served until 1907. He was the second Superintendent of VMI, and the first Superintendent who was a VMI graduate. He also served as a member of the Board of Visitors of the United States Military Academy at West Point, and was a member and President of the Board of Visitors of the United States Naval Academy. General Shipp was Superintendent Emeritus from 1907 until his death on 4 December 1917 in Lexington, Virginia, and was buried in the Stonewall Jackson Memorial Cemetery.

I.11. W. H. Cocke '94 Hall and the Memorial Garden

W. H. Cocke '94 Hall and the Memorial Garden are located between Jackson Memorial Hall and Scott Shipp Hall on Letcher Avenue, directly south of Old Barracks. When completed in 1927, the building was called '94 Hall, due to the significant donation from Superintendent Cocke who graduated from VMI in 1894. In 1938, when William Horner Cocke died, the building was renamed W. H. Cocke '94 ("Cocke") Hall. It was built primarily to provide a full gymnasium for the Corps, and was considered the largest in the South. It was also used for major dances ("Hops") at VMI, concerts, the annual commencement ceremony (before Cameron Hall was built), and a place where new cadets first matriculated (signed in).

Five gyms preceded Cocke Hall. The first gym (1848) was built in the arsenal basement; the second (1860), was a part of the mess hall; the third (1880's), was a frame building adjacent to Old Barracks; the fourth (1896), was in the basement of the first Jackson Memorial Hall; the fifth (1916), was in the basement of the second Jackson Memorial Hall; and the sixth (1927), was in '94 Hall. While another significant gymnasium was built and completed in 2016, and named the Corps Physical Training Facility, Cocke Hall is still used extensively by the cadets for intramural basketball games, an indoor track, a weight room and strength training facilities. In 2009, a new cardiovascular room was provided on the fifth floor of Cocke Hall with eight treadmills, four recumbent bikes, four upright bikes, six striders and four flat-screen TVs. In this room, the exercises reduce fat and improve the heart. The older cardiovascular room, located on the lower level near the weight room, still remains open.

The picture to the right is an aerial view of the back of Cocke Hall taken in 1938. It shows the huge size of this building compared to other buildings. The terraced garden and elliptical stairs leading down to the pedestrian bridge across Main Street were left of Cocke Hall and behind Jackson Memorial Hall were removed in 1969 for construction of an annex to the west end of Cocke Hall to

provide a new swimming pool. The annex was completed in 1970, substituting two pools for the pool which had been in use in Jackson Memorial Hall since 1916. The annex was named King Hall in 2007.

Cocke Hall is a contributing resource to the VMI Historic District. It is a masonry structure on a concrete foundation finished with painted stucco, stone trim, and a crenellated roof line. The rectangular building is 13-bays long with a flat roof supported by metal trusses, and skylights that allow natural light to enter the main gymnasium floor. The tall lancet-arched entrance is flanked by narrow octagonal turrets, reminiscent of those at the 1916 Jackson Memorial Hall next door, and includes double, glazed wood doors with Gothic panel details and large strap hinges, and incorporates a multi-pane window above the entrance. On both sides at the top of the lancet-arched entrance are decorations using shields set in trefoil panels. In addition to the skylights, the first floor is lit with glazed metal French doors, while upper levels have leaded metal casement sash windows with fixed transoms. The windows are single or set in clusters of two or three.

In 1939, a significant addition was made installing an indoor running track elevated above and surrounding the main floor. The Richmond architectural firm of Carneal, Johnston, and Wright donated its services for the planning and installation. Windows and other architectural elements were renovated in 2015 and 2016, but the historical significance was retained including the arrangement, proportioning, and design of the metal casement sash, French doors, skylights, and the raised indoor track. Both the exterior of Cocke Hall and the main gymnasium interior have retained excellent integrity.

Included in the Cocke Hall renovation in 2016 were spacious workout rooms on the lower floors where VMI wellness classes are held, with an entire floor devoted to locker and shower facilities, as well as the Charles S. Luck, Jr., '20 Memorial Weight Room, which was added in 1978. Luck was a 1920 VMI cadet. The original weight room was approximately 3,000 square feet, and was expanded in 1983.

Key renovations provided in 1995 and 2001 by Charles S. Luck, III, involved primarily the addition and enlargement of the dumbbell training area, which almost tripled in size and now contains weights ranging from five to 140 pounds. Auto-spot benches were installed, among the newest and safest pieces of weight training equipment available. New Olympic platforms were installed, with increased cushioning and padding for the weights. Four heavy-duty power racks, weighing 400 pounds each, were installed, and a number of back, leg, and neck machines were installed to complement existing equipment.

With over 7,000 square feet of space now, the Luck Weight Room contains over 40 separate pieces of resistive training machine-type equipment and over 70 pieces of free-weight training equipment with over 15,000 pounds of free weights and 2,000 pounds of dumbbell weights. VMI prides itself on providing each cadet with the tools to improve oneself not just intellectually, but physically. This facility can assist every cadet to reach maximum athletic potential.

Charles S. Luck, III

While Charles S. Luck, Jr., VMI Class of 1920, provided the initial funding in 1978 for the Luck Weight Room in Cocke Hall, his son Charles S. Luck, III, VMI Class of 1955, pictured to the right, provided more funding to renovate the Luck Weight Room. Luck III was very contributive to VMI serving on the VMI Alumni Association Board from 1965 to 1970, the VMI Board of Visitors from 1970 to 1978, the VMI Keydet Club Board from 1978 to 1981, and the VMI Foundation Board from 1987 to 1995.

Luck Stone Corporation has been in business for nearly a century as one of the largest producers of crushed stone, sand and gravel in the nation. Luck III was named president and CEO of Luck Stone in 1965, leading the company through three decades of expansion and innovation during his tenure. Before joining his father in the family business, Luck began his career after serving for two years in the U.S. Air Force. Luck III was a distinguished and honored businessman, serviceman, and civic leader born and raised in Richmond, Virginia. He has held numerous leadership positions in many of the industry trade associations and was instrumental in raising the environmental standards of the aggregates industry. He continues to participate in the Richmond community through various civic and non-profit organizations.

Memorial Garden

Memorial Garden was a gracious gift from Mrs. William Cocke in honor of her husband and her love for VMI on 12 June 1928, consisting of numerous plants, the Preston Parapet, a remarkable wall that included a public place for numerous plaques in memory of alumni who died in wars and other former cadets, and the symmetrical stairs.

At the ceremony, General Cocke formally presented the Garden to the Institute, and Robert Massie, Class of 1878 and president of the VMI Board of Visitors, received the gift on behalf of the Institute. In a brief address, Massie made a glowing tribute to Mrs. Cocke through whose efforts the Memorial Garden was made possible. It is also interesting that General Nichols, the third superintendent, who died almost a year before dedication of the Memorial Garden, was the object of a memorial service at Jackson Memorial Hall on the same day as the Memorial Garden ceremony.

The Memorial Garden is considered one of the most prominent open spaces on the VMI Post. It measures approximately 310 feet long and 90 feet wide, and is approximately 25 feet below the grade of Letcher Avenue. Changed significantly since its original dedication in 1928, the "Spirit of Youth" statue was mounted on the west side toward Jackson Memorial Hall in 1939 and, in 2017, the addition of a triple-arched memorial on the east end toward Scott Shipp Hall was placed with an inscription that reads: "In remembrance of all those who served the Institute." Two 10,000-gallon cisterns were installed below ground in the Garden in October 2016 as part of the Cocke Hall renovation collect rainwater to provide irrigation for the Garden plants and for use in the building's mechanical systems.

The Memorial Garden included a wide variety of distinctive plantings and species. Along the western edge, holly, rhododendron, pachysandra, and daffodils provided a setting for the "Spirit of Youth" statue, framed by large oak trees now removed. Along the eastern edge are yew and boxwood hedges, and dogwood trees. The front of Cocke Hall is framed by beds of pachysandra and cherry trees, and large masses of forsythia are along the north slope framing the monumental staircase.

General Cocke stated that the Memorial Garden would be dedicated to VMI men who served in various wars, but there were many more dedications. The Garden included four oak trees dedicated to the first four superintendents of VMI; a sun dial memorial for Commodore Matthew Fontaine Maury; a map which Commander Richard E. Byrd carried in his flight across the ocean; a rose bush and tablet in memory of Colonel T. 0. Smith; a bird bath was in memory of Colonel McDowell; a tablet dedicated by the Class of 1931 in memory of Cadets Cecil Edward West, Jr., and Thomas Milton Parrish, Jr., who died during their cadetship; a bronze tablet and box bush presented by members of the Class of 1931 to Cadet Edwin Amiss Palmer, Jr., who died during his cadetship; and eight cherry laurel trees previously planted by eight cadet captains, as symbols of victory, since the laurel was used in ancient times to crown war heroes. Most of these items were removed, and dedications to VMI cadets who died in a war now include plaques along the wall north of the Memoria Garden.

Bertram Goodhue, the second significant architect for VMI, designed in 1914 a grand central staircase to connect Old Barracks all the way to Main Street south of Letcher Avenue where there were no buildings on the undeveloped slope. As a result, the wall now north of the Memorial Garden with its symmetrical double stairs was considered an adaptation of Goodhue's 1914 architectural plan. In addition to the wall and stairs was the Memorial Garden and Cocke Hall filling the area between Jackson Memorial Hall and Scott Shipp Hall.

Preston Parapet

The parapet in Memorial Garden was prepared to honor J.T.L. Preston. This parapet, the wall with many plaques, the "Spirit of Youth" statue, and the triple-arched memorial on the East End contribute to the Memorial Garden's atmosphere of contemplative calm.

Alphabetical letters were added to the parapet to commemorate a quote from J.T.L. Preston, later called "The Father of VMI". Mrs. Cocke participated significantly in preparing for Memorial Garden and, for example, traveled to New York to see the Gorman Company, widely known silversmiths, for the purpose of obtaining the six-inch tall bronze inscription letters which were placed on the wall overlooking Memorial Garden. The inscription on the wall was from a statement published in the *Lexington Gazette* in 1835 written by Preston giving his vision of future VMI cadets.

"The healthful and pleasant abode of a crowd of honorable youths, pressing up the hill of science, with noble emulation, a gratifying spectacle, an honor to our country and our State, objects of honest pride to their instructors, and fair specimens of citizen-soldiers, attached to their native State, proud of her fame, and ready in every time of deepest peril to vindicate her honor, or defend her rights."

William Horner Cocke

Brigadier General William Horner Cocke was born on 28 September 1874 in Prince George County, Virginia. Cocke graduated from VMI in 1894, receiving the Institute's highest academic award, the Jackson-Hope Medal, First Honor. Between 1894 and 1897, he was the Commandant of Cadets and a professor of mathematics at Kemper Military Institute in Boonville, Missouri. Subsequently, he earned a law degree at Washington University in St. Louis where he practiced law. Cocke later served as a U. S. Army officer in both the Spanish-American War and World War I. In 1921, he founded in St. Louis the Southern Acid & Sulphur Company and headed that company that produced a refined yellow sulfur powder.

He became VMI's fourth Superintendent on 1 October 1924, holding the rank of Brigadier General in the Virginia National Guard. He resigned on 30 June 1929 due to his poor health after assuring himself that General John Lejeune was available to take over his position. He continued his support for VMI, however, as a member of the VMI Board of Visitors from 1930 to 1936.

When Cocke died on 9 June 1938 in Richmond, Virginia, it is notable that the VMI commencement program was canceled in order to honor Cocke for his many contributions to the Institute. General Charles Kilbourne, Superintendent at VMI, and members of the Board of Visitors attended the Cocke funeral at City Point, Virginia, where he was born, and his burial in Hopewell, Virginia.

Cocke donated generously from his personal funds to the Institute. His contribution for the construction of '94 Hall in 1927 was his largest gift, which also inspired significant contributions from his classmates. He also loaned funds to VMI in 1934 to purchase the Anderson House, which served as Alumni Hall until 1971. During his tenure, reconstruction of Letcher Avenue was begun, with concrete paving from Main Street up past the mess hall, and westward to the Post Gates. He also provided loans and gifts to aspiring faculty members to aid them in attaining graduate degrees.

In addition to Cocke's funding generosity, Robert Massie, president of the VMI Board of Visitors in 1939, when the "Spirit of Youth" statute was dedicated to Cocke in the Memorial Garden, felt the greatest service Cocke rendered VMI was due to its survival. Massie stated that a wave of pacifism swept over our country in 1928, leading the Virginia legislative Educational Committee to prepare a proposal with options to turn VMI over to its alumni and making it a private institution. Because the "pacifists" did not want military colleges, the proposal would eliminate

VMI from the State appropriations and distribute its appropriations to other colleges but, perhaps, allow VMI to convert to a vocational school. When Cocke became aware of the proposal, he immediately called the Board of Visitors, VMI alumni, and friends of VMI to come to Richmond and appear before the Educational Committee. It is reported that seldom has a more outraged citizenry stormed the State Capitol to shame those who would approve the recommendations. As a result, the recommendations were rejected by a vote of 72 to 15, thanks in large part to General Cocke, and VMI was conserved.

I.12. Clark King Hall

Clark King Hall is south of Letcher Avenue as an annex on the west side of Cocke Hall, constructed in 1970 at the rear of Jackson Memorial Hall, which required removal of the terraced steps and landscaping. It was first used for swim meets in the 1970-71 session.   Swimming had been in the Jackson Memorial basement since 1916. On 7 December 2007, the Cocke Hall annex was named in memory of Clark King.

The Clark King Pool is the principal element of the annex and has served as the home of the VMI Swimming and Diving program.   It has a six-lane swimming pool with spectator stands and dressing room facilities. Over the years, the Clark King Pool has undergone major improvements, including additions of a new scoreboard, record board, lane lines, and banners trumpeting the Conference Championships won in the program's history.   The annex has also provided the Institute's boxing ring and practice room, locker rooms and other facilities.

Clark King

Clark King was born in Amherst, Nebraska on 25 September 1923. A graduate of Nebraska State Teacher's College, King also earned a master's degree from the University of Wyoming and a Doctorate in Education from the University of Virginia. He was a Marine Corps officer in World War II from 1943 to 1946. He was awarded the Silver Star for gallantry in action on Iwo Jima in World War II, the Purple Heart, and a Presidential Unit Citation. After teaching chemistry and biology, and coaching football, basketball, and track at Blair High School in Nebraska, King was recalled to active duty during the Korean War. After his release from the Marines in 1952, he joined VMI as an assistant football coach.

King left active coaching in 1963 to succeed Herb Patchin (after his death) as VMI's Director of Physical Education, a position King held for 28 years until 1991. He became the first Director of Continuing Education in 1975 and also served as Director of the VMI Summer Session for many years. Dr. King was also a member of the faculty and staff from 1952 until his retirement in 1991, a member of the VMI Keydet Club Board from 1983 to 1989, and chairman of VMI's first Long Range Planning Committee.

From the 1970s, King was also active in VMI's drug and alcohol abuse education and prevention programs. He established the criteria for a mandatory course on alcohol and drug abuse. He received VMI's Distinguished Service Award in 1983 for his "extraordinary contributions to the life of the Institute". The founder of "Rat Training" (now known as "Rat Challenge"), King was honored in 1996 with the dedication of a new "high ropes" Rat Challenge training course. In 1997, King was elected an honorary alumnus of VMI by the Alumni Board and, on 6 December 1999.

In addition to his service at VMI, King was chairman of the Highway Safety Commission, on the House Mountain Development Committee, on the Lexington Board of Zoning Appeals, and involved in the development of the Chessie Trail along the east side of Maury River. He also served as vice-chairman of the Rockbridge Regional Jail Commission, on the Board of Trustees at Trinity United Methodist Church, and a member of the Lexington Kiwanis Club.

A VMI icon for fifty years, he died on 27 September 2002, at the age of 79 in Charlottesville, Virginia. He was buried in the Stonewall Jackson Memorial Cemetery in Lexington, Virginia. King stated that "Being trusted with the responsibility for teaching and training these young men is a high honor and very rewarding. When it is over, it is my hope that it mattered that I worked here."

I.13. Jackson Memorial Hall and VMI Museum

Jackson Memorial (JM) Hall is located on Letcher Avenue across from the southwest corner of Old Barracks. Completed in 1916, JM Hall was designed by Bertram Goodhue and named for Thomas "Stonewall" Jackson, who was a VMI faculty member and a general in the Confederate Army. JM Hall is significant for its architecture and was the first building constructed on the south slope of Letcher Avenue. JM Hall is a contributing historical building to the Virginia Military Institute Historic District.

The first floor assembly hall has been used every Sunday for chapel services, and was also used for graduation ceremonies, military commissions, class meetings, memorial services, and speeches by significant visitors. Circa 1920, a pool was constructed at the basement level and used for 50 years until a new swimming pool was built in an annex added to Cocke Hall in 1970, now named Clark King Hall. When use of the JM Hall swimming pool stopped, the VMI Museum was moved from Preston Library to a bottom floor in JM Hall. JM Hall also provided space for athletic functions below the main floor until Cocke Hall was built in 1927. The VMI Museum also housed the Hall of Valor, which commemorates the military war service of VMI alumni. It is now in Marshall Hall. In 2006, JM Hall completed major interior restoration at the lower level space which added a second floor to the VMI Museum.

JM Hall reflects the strong body of ecclesiastical architecture by Bertram Goodhue (1869-1924), who reinvigorated the Gothic Revival architectural style at VMI from 1914 to 1917, and the highly religious personality of Stonewall Jackson. JM Hall was Goodhue's most notable architecture at VMI, interior and exterior, with even attention to details such as the door hardware. It is the only non-residential, Goodhue-designed building completed at VMI.

The interior has a central nave rising two-and-a-half stories, lit by paired lancet windows in each of the balcony bays and the large lancet window above the front door. The nave is spanned by a flat, coffered wood ceiling, supported by simple curved brackets. The first floor assembly hall is designed as a romantic rustic character Gothic church interior with an exposed heavy timber structure that supports the upper side balconies. The east and west sides of the nave have timber-framed galleries for seats, low side aisles at the first floor level, and taller second floor galleries above.

JM Hall is significant with a seating capacity of about 1150, flags hanging below the ceiling that represent the 26 states in the Union when VMI was founded on 11 November 1839. Covering the wall behind the stage is a large work of art painted by Benjamin West Clinedinst, a member of the VMI class of 1880, depicting the VMI Cadet charge at the Battle of New Market on 15 May 1864. It was first unveiled on 24 June 1914 in the first JM Hall.

Benjamin West Clinedinst was born on 14 October 1859, in Woodstock, Virginia, and named after painter Benjamin West. After graduating from VMI, he studied for five years in Paris under famous painters Cabanel and Bonnat. He later attracted attention in New York City with his illustrations for *Leslie's Weekly*. In 1894, he was elected into the National Academy of Design as an Associate Academician, and became a full Academician in 1898. He was awarded the Evans prize of the American Watercolor Society in 1900. Clinedinst died on 12 September 1931, in Pawling, New York. In 1947 the nonprofit Artists' Fellowship, Inc. established the Benjamin West Clinedinst Memorial Medal for exceptional artistic merit.

The first JM Hall was built in 1896 and connected to Old Barracks north of Jackson Arch. In 1916, after completion of the second JM Hall, the Board of Visitors authorized razing the first JM Hall in order to complete Old Barracks as designed by A.J. Davis in 1850. The 1896 JM Hall was demolished in 1916, except for the three-bay central entry built over Jackson Arch in 1896.

Construction of the new JM Hall started in 1915 with $100,000 given to VMI by the federal government in recognition of damages to VMI inflicted by Union troops during the Civil War. The appropriation bill was initiated in 1913 by Senator Henry A. DuPont of Wilmington, Delaware after encouragement from Superintendent Nichols. The bill was passed in Congress and approved by President Woodrow Wilson. DuPont had applied for admission at VMI in 1855, but only Virginia boys were admitted, so duPont attended West Point. It is likely that a significant part of his motivation for the appropriation bill was his participation under General Hunter in the attack on VMI in the Civil War. Even in the attack, DuPont was upset.

Goodhue was a strong supporter of Davis and proposed demolition of the 1896 JM Hall in order to complete Old Barracks consistent with A.J. Davis. Prior to demolition of the 1896 JM Hall, Goodhue designed the new JM Hall and it was built on the steep hillside southwest of Old Barracks below Letcher Avenue. The design was correlated to Old Barracks with Gothic Revival features such as crenellations, buttresses, towers, Gothic arch windows, and leaded glass.

The present JM Hall has numerous parallels with the Cadet Chapel at West Point and other projects designed by Goodhue's firm. Details, such as hardware, found in the VMI building are very similar to Goodhue's earlier work. For example, the JM Hall entrance rim lock is almost identical to the rim lock at Saint Thomas's Church in New York City. In many ways, Goodhue adapted to VMI the concepts used at West Point. Significantly, JM Hall's imposing mass was set into the steep bluff just as the West Point Cadet Chapel was sited on a rocky cliff, with twin lancet windows, heavy buttresses, and traditional Gothic Revival detailing.

In addition to its construction on the steep slope, JM Hall has numerous parallels with the Cadet Chapel at West Point completed in 1910. The West Point Gothic Revival style church has a cruciform plan with a square Norman-style tower at its crossing, hexagonal towers at the entrance halll, and a crenellated roofline. The interior also has a long broad nave with low side aisles, and large and high windows that emphasize the structure and its verticality. It features a stone-vaulted ceiling and masonry floor with lancet-shaped stained glass windows.

JM Hall is a masonry structure supported by a concrete foundation. The front façade faces the Parade Ground and features a large central five-lancet Gothic arched window below a prominent pediment flanked by short octagonal towers. The central nave portion has a front-gabled roof covered with standing seam metal roofing and there are two small slot type windows in each turret. Set below a heavy basket-handle arch are the double entrance doors. The doors have vertical tongue-and-groove boards and heavy-cast iron strap hinges. The original rim lock hardware, imprinted with the VMI crest, remains on the interior side designed by Goodhue. The exterior is coated with painted stucco and limestone trim detailing. The three-story building is eight-bays long and one-bay wide, and the side elevations feature twin lancet windows in each turret between heavy buttresses. The parapet walls are crenellated. On the west façade, a staircase leads from the Parade Ground level to Cocke Hall Annex.

The picture taken from Memorial Garden shows the east side of JM Hall. The east and west facades rise three-and-a-half stories with buttresses between each window bay. The upper lancet arched windows are paired, with pyramid-arched leaded glass windows and limestone surrounds. The windows at ground level are covered with  limestone basket-handle arches. Secondary entrances are located on the east and west facades at the top level. In 2006, a direct pedestrian route was constructed into the east side of JM Hall along the Memorial Garden wall.

In 1929, a pedestrian bridge was constructed across Main Street, leading from the south side of JM Hall to the Alumni Memorial Field. In conjunction with this work, a terraced garden was created behind JM Hall. As shown in a 1938 aerial image, the garden was laid out with two tiers of limestone retaining walls and curved symmetrical staircases on the east and west. The staircases framed the terraces on both sides and two trees framed the passage to the pedestrian bridge. A third garden tier was added in 1937 with four tall and narrow trees. Construction of the Cocke Hall annex in 1970 eliminated the historic terraced landscape garden and elliptical stairways which existed between the rear of JM Hall and Main Street.

Thomas Jonathan "Stonewall" Jackson

"Stonewall" Jackson was born in Clarksburg, Virginia (now West Virginia) on 21 January 1824, and died on 10 May 1863 at the age of 39 at Guinea Station, Virginia. He was buried in Lexington, Virginia, at the Presbyterian Church Cemetery, which was renamed the Stonewall Jackson Memorial Cemetery in the 1920's.

Jackson had a difficult childhood. His father died in 1826 when Jackson was only two, and his mother died in 1831 when he was seven. As a result, he lived with several uncles until he was accepted and left for West Point. He graduated 17th out of 59 graduates in 1846 despite his previous poor schooling experience.

After graduation, Jackson was a second lieutenant in the U.S. Army and fought in the Mexican-American War from 1846-48. It was in Mexico that Jackson met Robert E. Lee. After the war, Jackson served at several Army bases, but was discontent with his experience. As a result, he applied to be in the VMI faculty and was accepted in 1851. He was professor of Natural and Experimental Philosophy, and instructor of Artillery, which he had experienced in the Mexican-American War. While Jackson was an outstanding artillery instructor, he was unpopular as a philosophy professor and a group of alumni attempted to have him removed from the faculty. Obviously he was not.

After joining VMI, Jackson was also a member and deacon of the Lexington Presbyterian Church, and chose to organize Sunday afternoon classes for young African-Americans at the Presbyterian Church. His second wife, Mary Anna Jackson, taught with Jackson, stating in one of her books that "he preferred that my labors should be given to the colored children, believing that it was important and useful to put the strong hand of the Gospel under the African race, to lift them up." Jackson's pastor, Dr. William Spotswood White was also an African-American and described the relationship between Jackson and his Sunday afternoon students: "In their religious instruction he succeeded wonderfully. His discipline was systematic and firm, but very kind. His servants reverenced and loved him, as they would have done a brother or father. He was emphatically the black man's friend." He addressed his students by name and they referred to him affectionately as "Marse Major" with "Marse" meaning "Master".

At VMI, Jackson became close with John Thomas Lewis Preston when Jackson married Elinor Junkin, the sister of Preston's wife. They worked together on the VMI faculty and Preston helped teach Sunday School for African-American children. Preston was on Jackson's staff during the Civil War.

After ten years on the VMI faculty, the Civil War began in 1861 and, on 27 April 1861, Virginia Governor John Letcher ordered Colonel Jackson as a Virginia Militia to take command at Harpers Ferry, where he would assemble and command the unit which later gained fame as the "Stonewall Brigade", consisting of the 2nd, 4th, 5th, 27th, and 33rd Virginia Infantry regiments. All of these units were from the Shenandoah Valley region of Virginia, where Jackson located his headquarters throughout the first two years of the war. Jackson became known for his relentless drilling of his troops, believing that discipline was vital to success on the battlefield. Following victorious raids on the Union B&O Railroad on 24 May, he was promoted to Brigadier General on 17 June 1861.

Jackson quickly rose to prominence and earned his famous nickname "Stonewall" at the First Battle of Bull Run (First Manassas) on 21 July 1861. As the Confederate lines began to crumble under heavy Union assault, Jackson's brigade provided crucial reinforcements on Henry House Hill, demonstrating the discipline he instilled in his men. Brigadier General Barnard Elliott Bee Jr. exhorted his own troops to re-form by shouting, "There is Jackson standing like a stone wall. Rally behind the Virginians!" Jackson's brigade, which would afterwards be known as the Stonewall Brigade, stopped the Union assault that day, and he was then called "Stonewall Jackson". After the battle, Jackson was promoted to Major General on 7 October 1861 and given command of the Shenandoah Valley District, with headquarters in Winchester.

In the summer of 1862, Jackson and his troops were called to join Robert E. Lee's Army of Northern Virginia to defend Richmond against the Union General McClellan's Peninsula Campaign. Utilizing a railroad tunnel under the Blue Ridge Mountains designed by Claudius Crozet, Jackson's troops were transported to Hanover County on the Virginia Central Railroad, and his forces made a surprise appearance in front of McClellan at Mechanicsville. This made a crucial factor in McClellan's decision to retreat and end the Peninsula Campaign.

When Lee decided to invade the North in the Maryland Campaign, Jackson hastened to join Robert E. Lee's Army of Northern Virginia at Sharpsburg, Maryland, where they fought McClellan again in the Battle of Antietam (Sharpsburg). Antietam was a battle against superior Union soldiers , and Lee withdrew the Army of Northern Virginia back across the Potomac River, ending the invasion. On 10 October 1962, Jackson was promoted to Lieutenant General, being ranked just behind Robert E. Lee and James Longstreet, and his command was assigned to the Second Corps.

Jackson fought in other battles including the Second Battle of Bull Run, the Battle of Fredericksburg and others, but his last was the Battle of Chancellorsville when the Confederate Army of Northern Virginia was faced with a serious threat by the Union Army of the Potomac and its new commanding general, Major General Joseph Hooker. Jackson and his entire corps went on an aggressive flanking maneuver to the right of the Union lines, and employed Major General Fitzhugh Lee's cavalry to provide reconnaissance regarding the exact location of the Union right and rear. They later rode together to view the enemy. Jackson immediately returned to his corps on 2 May 1863 and arranged his divisions into a line of battle to charge directly into the Union army. The Confederates marched silently until they were only several hundred feet from the Union position, when they released a bloodthirsty cry and full charge. Many of the Federals were captured without a shot fired, while the rest were driven into a full rout.

Darkness ended the assault. As Jackson and his staff were returning to camp, they were mistaken by the 18th North Carolina Infantry to be a Union cavalry force regiment. They shouted, "Halt, who goes there?", but fired before the reply. Jackson was hit by three bullets, two in the left arm and one in the right hand. Several other men in his staff were killed, in addition to many horses. Darkness and confusion prevented Jackson from getting immediate care.

Because of his injuries, Jackson's left arm had to be amputated by Dr. Hunter McGuire and Jackson was moved to Thomas Chandler's plantation named *Fairfield* in Guinea Station, Virginia. Jackson was offered Chandler's home for recovery, but Jackson refused and suggested using Chandler's plantation office building instead. He was thought to be out of harm's way but, unknown to the doctors, he already had classic symptoms of pneumonia, complaining frequently of a sore chest. Jackson died of  complications from pneumonia on 10 May 1863, eight days after he was shot. Jackson played a prominent role in nearly all military engagements in the Civil War until his untimely death, and played an important part in winning many significant battles.

Upon hearing of Jackson's death, Robert E. Lee mourned the loss of both a friend and a trusted commander. The night Lee learned of Jackson's death, he told his cook: "William, I have lost my right arm, and I'm bleeding at the heart." After the war, Jackson's wife and young daughter Julia moved from Lexington to North Carolina. Mary Anna Jackson wrote two books about her husband's life, including some of his letters. She never remarried, and was known as the "Widow of the Confederacy", living until 1915. His daughter Julia married and bore children, but she died of typhoid fever at the age of 26 years.

Jackson has been commemorated on U.S. postage stamps on three occasions. The first was a commemorative stamp that also honored Robert E. Lee, issued in 1936. The second stamp issued in 1970 was in conjunction with the dedication of the Stone Mountain Confederate Memorial carving in Georgia and included Lee and Jefferson Davis. A third stamp commemorating Jackson was released in 1995.

Jackson was also commemorated in a stained glass in the Washington National Cathedral honoring his service in the Mexican-American War and there is also a stained glass window honoring Jackson in the Fifth Avenue Presbyterian Church in Roanoke, Virginia. The window in Roanoke was supported by an African-American, Reverend Downing, whose parents were taught by Stonewall Jackson in Lexington. The stained glass still remains behind the pulpit in the church and depicts a quote from Jackson stated soon before he died: "Let Us Cross the River and Rest in the Shade of the Trees".

Several statues were sculpted for Jackson. Curiously, the first was provided by English donors who gave the statue of "Stonewall" Jackson, sculptured by John Henry Foley, to the Commonwealth of Virginia in 1875 and placed in the Capital Square in Richmond, Virginia. Extra funds led to the Jackson-Hope Medal at VMI. A Jackson statue was placed on his grave in Lexington's Stonewall Jackson Memorial Cemetery in 1895. One was also placed in the West Virginia capital in 1910, as he was born in Virginia (now West Virginia). It was sculpted by Moses Ezekiel, who graduated from VMI in the class of 1867. A replica of this statue was dedicated at VMI on 19 June 1912 and unveiled by Anna Jackson Preston, only twenty-two months old, the great-granddaughter of both General Jackson and John Thomas Lewis Preston.

VMI Museum

The VMI Museum has been located in Jackson Memorial Hall since artifacts were moved from Preston Library in 1970 after a new swimming pool was built in the Cocke Hall annex and open space was created in the basement of JM Hall by clearing the exercise room and no longer using the swimming pool. In 1964, another museum was added at the New Market Battlefield, and another museum was created in 2011 at the Stonewall Jackson House in Lexington.

The VMI Museum collects, preserves, interprets, and exhibits the heritage of VMI as recorded in the 15,000 artifact collection. The museum is professionally accredited by the American Association of Museums, and is directed by Colonel Keith Gibson, VMI Class of 1977. All the objects have been cataloged with accession numbers that are stored in a computerized database. The artifacts themselves are stored in acid-free boxes under climate-controlled conditions with a high security system. The museum also contains a reference library and conference room where classes can meet and artifacts can be used to enhance lectures.

The museum in JM Hall now fills two floors. The upper museum floor opened provides the history of VMI. As one walks into the museum, the room exhibits the counter, artifacts, books and VMI elements for sale.

On the other side of this room, one will see "Little Sorrel", "Stonewall" Jackson's favorite horse, and Jackson's portrait. In front, there are seven Medals of Honor which have been awarded to VMI alumni. The museum's items chronicle the story of the nation's first state-sponsored military college.

Directly across from the Jackson display is a full-scale furnished replica of a cadet's room complete racks, furniture, uniforms and books.

A VMI class ring exhibit is also displayed in the museum, with the earliest ring from 1848, and an unbroken lineage of rings since 1913. The beautiful ring below with "Stonewall" Jackson, Virginia Mourning her Dead, and the blue sapphire gemstone of wisdom and tranquility was from my class of 1965, in which I was a member of the of the Ring Committee.

The lower floor was restored in 2006, and displays the Henry M. Stewart antique firearms collection and the Kohen Gallery, donated by Margot and Joseph B. Kohen, Jr., VMI Class of 1950B, which has significant portraits and clothing.

The idea for a museum was initiated in 1845 by a letter from Superintendent Smith to a small number of VMI alumni requesting that they "collect Curiosities, both literary and natural, the collection and deposit of which might form the commencement of a MUSEUM." Smith added in his letter that a gun lock picked up on the plains of Jamestown was presented to him, and used by the first settlers of Virginia as early as 1607. Smith added that the alumni may possess some historical traditions or documents, which might throw additional light upon the early history of Virginia and our country. With the acceptance of a Revolutionary War rifle, a powder horn, and a bullet pouch in 1856, Superintendent Smith created the VMI Museum making it the oldest museum in Virginia. In 1862, many construction plans, including an Agricultural and Mineral Specimens Museum, were cancelled due to the Civil War.

Until the first 1907 library building was built, all artifacts were located in Old Barracks. In 1908, the librarian Miss Nellie Gibbs collected the artifacts from Old Barracks and arranged them in the 1907 Library building which became the core of the VMI Museum. The museum was a part of the 1907 Library until 1932 when the museum artifacts were moved into the new Nichols Engineering Hall and, then, into the Preston Library after it opened in November 1939. Pictured

to the right are artifacts moved to the museum in JM Hall from a museum room in the Preston Library which is now the Dolly Turman Room and includes portraits of all the VMI Superintendents.

Many items in the museum collection have been presented over the past 140 years by individuals who used them. For example, WWII General George Patton, VMI Class of 1907 penned a note "One of my VMI web belts Mama kept" sent to VMI with his VMI web belt. Also, a quilt created by Mary Custis Lee was donated to the VMI Museum in 1926. The museum traces the careers of many alumni, with museum contributions from Nobel Prize recipients, Pulitzer Prize winners, explorers, film stars, national, state and local political and civic leaders.

I.14. NICHOLS HALL

Nichols Hall, formerly known as the Nichols Engineering Building, is located south of Letcher Avenue between the Preston Library and Jackson Memorial Hall. It was named for the third VMI superintendent Lieutenant General Edward West Nichols and has served as an academic building for the Engineering Department since it was originally completed in 1931, and houses VMI's Civil and Environmental, Electrical, and Mechanical Engineering Departments as well as the Department of Information System Technology and the Geology classroom. The building also included the Superintendent's office until Smith Hall was built in 1964.

Nichols Hall was designed by the firm of Carneal and Johnston in Richmond, Virginia, to harmonize with the Gothic architectural theme at VMI. William Leigh Carneal was a VMI graduate in the Class of 1903. Two annexes were added to the west and south facades of the original building circa 1960, and the engineering hall underwent a complete renovation in 2005. An annex was added to the building in 1959, and named Morgan Hall in 2007. Nichols Hall is a contributing resource to the VMI Historic District.

The original building is a concrete structure five-stories tall, with a central entrance bay marked by shallow and square crenellated turrets and arched main entrance. Only three stories are visible from the Parade Ground. The original Nichols Hall building is coated with painted stucco and decorated with cast stone trim. It was the first academic building constructed to the west of Jackson Memorial Hall along Letcher Avenue. The monument statue of *Virginia Mourning her Dead* is located in a memorial plaza immediately in front of Nichols Hall.

EDWARD WEST NICHOLS

Lieutenant General Edward West Nichols was born in Petersburg, Virginia, on 27 June 1858. Nichols graduated from VMI in 1878 and served VMI as an assistant instructor for three years. He studied law at Washington & Lee University and the University of Virginia. After practicing law for one year, he returned to the Institute in 1882, accepting the Chair of Engineering. Nichols was subsequently a professor of mathematics and civil engineering at the Institute, and wrote textbooks on analytical geometry and calculus.

On 1 July 1907, he was the Acting Superintendent, and became VMI's third Superintendent on 30 June 1908. One of his most important roles was hiring Bertram Goodhue in 1913, the second best VMI architect who completed Old Barracks, designed three faculty houses on Parade Avenue, expanded the Parade Ground extensively, and designed Jackson Memorial Hall.

From 1918-1919, Nichols was an officer in the U. S. Army Corps of Engineers and was commander of the Student Army Training Corps at VMI. Following his retirement as Superintendent on 30 September 1924, he continued to lecture in Pure and Applied Mathematics, and was named Superintendent Emeritus. He died three years later on 1 July 1927 at the age of 69, as the result of a rock blasted during the construction of duplex quarters at 402/404 VMI Parade site near his home at the Superintendent's Quarters. He was buried in the Stonewall Jackson Memorial Cemetery. Almost a year later on 12 June 1928, a memorial service was held for Nichols at Jackson Memorial Hall on the same day as the VMI Memorial Garden dedication ceremony.

I.15. Morgan Hall

Morgan Hall is an annex south of Letcher Avenue located behind Nichols Hall. The picture shows the Morgan name over the tunnel, with the Morgan annex on the left. The annex was built in 1959 and was extensively renovated on 2006. The annex was dedicated on 13 February 2007 in honor of former VMI Dean Major General James M. Morgan Jr., VMI Class of 1945.

Formerly known as the Nichols Engineering Building Annex, Morgan Hall houses laboratories and classrooms for many of the Civil and Environmental Engineering courses taught at the Institute. At the dedication of Morgan Hall in 2007, General J.H. Binford Peay III, the VMI Superintendent and a member of the Class of 1962 when he majored in Civil Engineering as one of Morgan's students, said "General Morgan was always the consummate gentleman and a very fine teacher. His leadership has had a lasting impact on VMI, and so it is appropriate that this facility be named in his honor."

James M. Morgan, Jr.

James Morgan was born in Richmond, Virginia, on 11 August 1923. He entered VMI in 1941 with the class of 1945, resigning in 1943 to enter the armed forces. Returning to VMI in 1944, he graduated in 1946 having served as First Captain of the Corps of Cadets and as a member of the Honor Court and General Committee. Also, he was a distinguished graduate of the Institute and holder of VMI's two highest graduation honors, the Jackson-Hope Medal, First Honor for academic achievement, and the Society of the Cincinnati Medal for leadership and all-round excellence.

Morgan joined the VMI faculty in the fall of 1946 and served 38 years at VMI. He began teaching as a civil engineer instructor and began graduate study at Johns Hopkins University, where he earned a master's degree in environmental engineering and a doctorate in civil engineering. In 1955, he was promoted to colonel, professor of civil engineering and head of the Civil Engineer Department. Also in 1955, he joined the VMI Foundation Board and remained there for 10 years until 1965. In 1965, Morgan became dean of the faculty and retired from that position in 1984. He was also the first director of the VMI Research Laboratories. Additional duties he fulfilled at VMI included serving as an assistant commandant, 1949-1953, and as the superintendent's representative to the Honor Court.

The announcement of Morgan's retirement was made by Superintendent General Sam S. Walker, and they were Brother Rats. Walker expressed deep regret for Morgan's retirement, stating they were lifelong friends. Walker also stated: "His entire professional life has been spent in dedicated service to VMI, and I am comforted that General Morgan has agreed to be available for consultation and that he will continue to teach part-time and assist part-time in the Department of Civil Engineering. I know all of the members of the VMI family join me in expressing our most sincere appreciation for the quality and significance of his service."

Also a member of the U.S. Army Reserve for 33 years, he retired in 1981 as a colonel after serving in the Office of the Surgeon General as the sanitary engineer for 14 years. He was a graduate of the U.S. Army Associate Command and General Staff College, and a holder of the Legion of Merit and the Meritorious Service Medal with an oak leaf cluster. Morgan worked in numerous other activities, serving in leadership and board positions with the Virginia Section of the American Society of Civil Engineers, the Lynchburg Chapter of the Virginia Society of Professional Engineers, the Stonewall Jackson Hospital, the Virginia State Board of Health (appointed by Governor Mills E. Godwin), the United Virginia Bank, and other organizations. He had the longest tenure of academic deans among Virginia's colleges and universities and was chairman of the Virginia Council of Academic Vice Presidents. He also performed extensive research for the Atomic Energy Commission in the disposal of radioactive wastes and other projects.

Engaged often in research, Morgan published scholarly and professional articles and is the author of a book on the Jackson-Hope and Society of Cincinnati Medals and co-author with Brother Rat James L. Morrison Jr. about Garry Owen: "The Horse at VMI". He was also a member of the Kappa Alpha Order. When asked what his service at VMI meant to him, Morgan replied, "I look back on three very pleasant experiences: First, the collegiality of a very dedicated VMI faculty; second, the opportunity to serve under six of the eleven VMI superintendents; and, thirdly, the thousands of VMI cadets who have matriculated since the days of my cadetship have taught me much more than I ever taught them".

I.16. Preston Library

Preston Library is located on the south side of Letcher Avenue between Nichols Hall and Mallory Hall. Its construction was completed in 1939 and named for Colonel John Thomas Lewis Preston, who has been called the "Father of VMI". The highlight of the Preston Library dedication was a congratulatory

speech by President Roosevelt on a telephone connected to the public address system. The Preston Library has served as VMI's main library from its original construction to the present, and was carefully designed to complement the existing Gothic Revival buildings at VMI. Preston Library is a contributing resource to the VMI Historic District.

The Preston Library is a concrete structure with an exterior veneer of painted stucco and cast stone trim. The rectangular building has a tall central section with lower, flanking wings. Overall, the building is five stories tall, though only three stories are visible from the Parade Ground. The low roof parapet walls are crenellated. From the Parade Ground, large vent hoods can be seen along the west roof. Preston's Parade Ground façade has a central entrance bay which dominates the building. Flanked by octagonal turrets, it features a carved limestone panel with surrounded multiple windows and an arched entrance.

The main entrance has four paneled doors set under a basket-handle arch. Each door has a small grille, large metal pull, and decorative nail heads. The main entrance is accessed by a small concrete bridge, which spans across an areaway that runs along the north side of the building. The heavy masonry massing is emphasized by wide buttresses set between window bays in the flanking wings.

The window panes are typically clustered in groups of three. Each window unit consists of a metal eighteen-light casement sash with a lower fixed three-light window and a six-light transom above. The east and west facades have two-story bay windows with decorative cast stone panels. The new rear addition of Preston Library completed in 1972, is a three-story tall, seven-bay wide stucco-covered masonry building. The flat-roofed addition is not visible from the Parade Ground. The entire facility underwent a major renovation in 1996.

The interior of the Preston Library has some remaining historical finishes in the entrance lobby and stairwells. The entrance lobby has remnants of stone arches. Original stairwells are steel with wood handrails and terrazzo treads. The railings and newel posts have Gothic arched detailing. Significant improvements occurred in the 1980's with the advice of Joseph Neikirk. These included the Periodicals Room (1980), the Dolly Hardee Turman Rare Book Room (1982), the new circulation area with improved lighting (1985), and the audiovisual center (1987). The Library installed an integrated library system in 1991 and upgraded its system in 2004.

The mission of Preston Library is to provide library materials and services of the highest quality; to teach skills needed for academic inquiry and lifelong learning; to support faculty and undergraduate research; to provide access to and promote the use of Institute historical materials; to support the creation and use of multimedia by cadets and faculty; and to offer library services to the community-at-large. The library provides resources for study and research by cadets and faculty, support for the VMI Archives, and the repository of the Institute's historic records.   The archives were separated from the rare book room in 1978 and now occupy separate quarters in the library. The early contents of the archives were publicized in a book named "*A Virginia Military Institute Album, 1839-1910*" by archivist Diane B. Jacob, who is still director of the VMI archives. The Archives Office contains VMI's historic official records, photographs, manuscripts, rare materials, and a digital website.

Preston Library's collections include over 300,000 volumes of printed materials, over 5000 non-printed items, and more than 300 scientific, literary, and general interest printed periodicals. The online catalog is available at library.vmi.edu. In addition, the library provides access to more than 100 full-text and citation databases and over 60,000 full-text electronic journals, many purchased through VIVA (the Virtual Library of Virginia). Preston Library is a selective depository of U.S. government publications, with current holdings of about 200,000 federal and state documents. Inter-library loan service is available to cadets and faculty free of charge. Preston Library provides wireless access to the library on-line at www.vmi.edu/library.

The building is equipped with 32 public-access, networked computers for research use, and a computer instruction lab which enables librarians to offer hands-on training for our numerous online resources. Preston Library also has 110 individual small cubicles with desks that are available on a first come, first serve basis. The cubicles are equipped with study lamps, power outlets, and network connections. There are six group study rooms available on the 6th floor in addition to many large tables for study and research.

Media Services has 18 media cubicles, a media creation room, and a media projection room for classes to view video formats. In addition, the library maintains a music collection with music players and comfortable seating in the Timmins Music Room. Each floor also has a gallery area furnished with comfortable armchairs and sofas.

The history of the VMI libraries is extensive. The first library was recommended in 1839 by the Virginia State Librarian William H. Richardson. His interest in VMI continued for many years and he had the first library books sent to VMI from Richmond in September 1840. Richardson also proposed a resolution to the Virginia Assembly that appropriated $500 per year for five years to VMI for its library. By the end of 1840, a new wing with three stories had been built on the east side of the old Virginia Militia barracks, and one of the rooms on the third floor was used as the first library. In 1844, the library room was moved to the second floor of the old arsenal's gun and ammunition house closely north of the barracks.

In the early 1850's, John Letcher, a congressman for the Rockbridge district, used his influence that enabled Federal government publications to be added to the VMI library. In 1854, faculty member Thomas Williamson was appointed librarian, and created the first catalogue of the library books. Following progress, almost 10,000 books were destroyed when barracks were burned by the Union Army in 1864. After the Civil War when the barracks were reconstructed, six former cadet rooms in Old Barracks next to and south of Jackson Arch housed the library in 1868, which extended upward for two stories with a balcony around the second floor.

VMI had the Society of Cadets and the Dialectic Society, which had their own libraries. The Society of Cadets was formed in the winter of 1839-40 with encouragement from Superintendent Smith for public speaking experience and the group was named after cadets at West Point. The Dialectic Society was added in 1848 for conversation and debating, and all cadets were eligible for membership. It is reported that both Societies ended about 1909.

In 1897, the library was moved from Old Barracks into the first Jackson Memorial Hall which was added to the west side of Old Barracks, north of Jackson Arch. To the right is an interior view of the Library in 1898. This view shows the book stacks and several portraits, including the large portrait of Superintendent Smith.

Ten years later, in 1907, a new building was built outside of the northwest end of Barracks

to provide a large library, and was the VMI Library until the Preston Library was built in 1939. The 1907 Library building was constructed on the site now occupied by New Barracks, and was a three-story stuccoed masonry building with a central four-story square tower and a five-story building attached to the rear. The second floor was occupied by faculty quarters and included a new meeting room for the VMI Board of Visitors. On the top floor was a large room used by the Dialectic Society, and also used for drawing and other classes. The library was a side-gabled three-story. The library was demolished in 1948 to make room for New Barracks.

The books had increased significantly as 14,850 were transferred to the new 1907 library.   The new librarian from 1908 until 1928 was Miss Nellie Gibbs. In addition to her library duties, she collected and arranged the artifacts which became the core of the VMI Museum, and the museum was a part of the library until 1932 when it was moved into the new Nichols Engineering Hall.

John Thomas Lewis Preston

Preston was born on 25 April 1811 in Lexington, Virginia.   He was the fourth descendent of John Preston, of Augusta County, the progenitor of a family noted in America for the number of illustrious Preston men produced. J.T.L. Preston was raised in Richmond and Lexington, and received his education at Washington College (now Washington and Lee University), and later the University of Virginia.

For more than a half a century, Preston was a commanding and leading figure in the life of nineteenth-century Lexington. His addresses in favor of the proposition to establish a military school at Lexington in meetings of the Franklin society – then the center of intellectual discourse in the community – were instrumental in persuading state and local leaders to realize his vision of a first class college in a military setting. His efforts resulted in the foundation of Virginia Military Institute on 11 November 1839, and the Preston Parapet in the Memorial Garden states his vision of the VMI cadets. He was chosen to be the only professor of languages and rhetoric at VMI upon its establishment, and continued to serve the VMI until 1882. He was also a member of VMI's Board of Visitors in 1839 and from 1856 to 1857.

The only interruption for his term as a professor was during the Civil War (1861-65). At the opening of the war he was commissioned a lieutenant colonel in the 9th Virginia Infantry, and in the fall of that year he was assigned to duty as aide-de-camp to General Stonewall Jackson.

For 59 years he was a member of the Lexington Presbyterian Church and for 47 years a ruling elder. He was a man of strong and unwavering religious faith, a thorough student of the Gospel Scriptures, and extensively read in theological works. In cooperation with Stonewall Jackson and his wife from 1855 to 1961, he conducted a Sunday school for African-American children, both free and enslaved, at the Lexington Presbyterian Church.

Preston was married twice. In 1832, he first married Sarah Lyle Carothers. After her death, he married Margaret Junkin in 1857, the sister of Stonewall Jackson's first wife, Elinor Junkin. Margaret Junkin Preston, daughter of a president of Washington College, was a major, nineteenth century literary figure, known nationally as the "Poetess of the South." Their magnificent home on Preston Street in Lexington, past the southern end of Lee Avenue, has been preserved intact to the present.

Preston died in Lexington, Virginia on 15 July 1890, and was buried in the Stonewall Jackson Memorial Cemetery. Again, he was the "Father of VMI, and died four months after the death of the first VMI Superintendent Francis Smith.

I.17. Mallory Hall

Mallory Hall is located on Letcher Avenue along the south side of the Parade Ground, between Preston Library and Maury-Brook Hall, and named for Brigadier General Francis Mallory, a long-time VMI professor of physics and electrical engineering. It was the first academic building to be constructed in the post-WWII years, completed in September 1952. Mallory Hall initially housed the Mathematics and Physics Departments and, now, includes Astronomy and Computer Science. In the autumn of 1960, the Atomic Energy Commission granted funds for a subcritical nuclear reactor, which was installed in Mallory Hall in 1961. It was a great asset to the Physics Department and to its nuclear physics laboratory.

The main façade facing the Parade Ground is two-stories tall with a central bay embellished with multi-paned arched windows and carved limestone surround. The main entrance is accessed by a small concrete bridge that spans the lower ground level in front of the building. A two-story, rectangular addition was constructed at the southeast corner of the original structure in 1960, designed in the Gothic style to harmonize with the other buildings on the Post. In 1989, Mallory Hall was connected to the new science building, now named Maury-Brooke Hall, and major renovations occurred in 2008. The building now has a large number of classrooms, offices, laboratories, and two large lecture/demonstration rooms. The top level is now home to VMI's Department of Applied Mathematics. Mallory Hall is a contributing building to the VMI Historic District.

Francis Mallory

Francis Mallory was born in Norfolk, Virginia, on 15 April 1868. He graduated from Norfolk Academy in 1886 and from VMI in 1889, with a degree in Civil Engineering, the last year Francis Smith was the superintendent. At graduation, Mallory was also the winner of the Second Honor Jackson-Hope Medal.

After graduation from VMI, he was commandant and professor of mathematics at the Fishburne Military Academy in Waynesboro, Virginia from 1889 to 1891, and then returned to VMI as the Post Adjutant and assistant professor of mathematics from 1891 to 1894. He then began postgraduate studies in physics, mathematics, and astronomy at the University of Chicago and received his Doctor of Science Degree from John Hopkins University in 1897.

An adjunct professor of physics and astronomy at VMI from 1897 to 1899, Mallory organized and directed the electrical engineering curriculum in 1899 and physics became a separate curriculum course in 1921. Mallory was a professor of physics and electrical engineering at VMI from 1899 to 1940. This long tenure explains why Mallory Hall was named for him, and he was regarded as the man who had come into contact with more cadets than anyone in the Institute's history. Mallory loved physics and all cadets had to take at least a year of physics until that requirement was dropped after World War II.

As a senior faculty member, Mallory lived in the Gilham House (now Maury House) on the VMI Parade street. An outstanding teacher, he was also a disciplinarian with a quote "If you don't work my problems, I bull ya." This was a well-remembered phrase of the "little man with a big backbone". Mallory also served with Colonel Pendleton to perform the superintendent's functions for about a year after September 1932, when Superintendent General Lejeune was walking on a steep hillside behind Old Barracks to look at the work in progress on Richardson Hall when he slipped, fell down the hill, and was incapacitated for about a year.

At Finals in April 1939, Mallory presented his resignation to the VMI Board of Visitors, but they declined to accept it, preferring to retain him as Head of the Physics Department but relieving him of the responsibility of teaching. He was named professor emeritus and promoted to Brigadier General, a rank which he had previously resisted. At the same time, he delivered the VMI Centennial address, which was an appropriate assignment for the man who was a cadet and teacher who had served VMI for almost 50 years and taught more cadets than any other person.

In 1941, Mallory retired from VMI due to ill health and died in Lexington on 12 August 1943 at the age of 75. At his death, his doctor was his son, Brooke Baylor Mallory, with names fror his mother. Brooke Mallory matriculated at VMI in 1925, left VMI after two years in 1927 to attend West Point, returned to VMI in 1929, and graduated from VMI in th Class of 1930 with a degree in chemistry. Afterwards, he attended medical school at the University of Virginia, graduated with his doctor's degree in 1934, and returned to VMI in 1936 as the assistant surgeon. After the surgeon died the following year, Brooke was appointed as the VMI Post Surgeon and commissioned as a major in the Virginia Volunteers. After his father's death in 1941, he was ordered to report to Fort Belvoir, Virginia, for active duty in the United States Army Medical Corps.

I.18. Maury-Brooke Hall

A new Science Building was completed at VMI in 1988 west of Mallory Hall and the initial Post Limits Gate (in the picture), and south of Letcher Avenue. It was named for scientists Matthew Fontaine Maury and John Mercer Brooke in 2010 because it is an academic building for chemistry and biology curriculums. A former building used for chemistry east of Old Barracks was named for Maury-Brooke from 1909 to 2010. In 2010, that older building, which now houses the registrar's office, the band instruments, and military store operations, was renamed Shell Hall. The lives of these scientists Maury and Brooke intersected more than once. Both helped connect America and Europe with the first transatlantic telegraph cable, probed the movement and depth mysteries of the oceans while at the U.S. Naval Observatory, served the Confederate Navy during the Civil War, and after the Civil War spent the rest of their careers on the VMI faculty.

In 1988, the Science Building construction resulted in the demolition of several historic cottages at that site, including one built for John Williamson in 1867. Fortunately, the Pendleton-Coles House, now the VMI Admissions Office, was not demolished but moved westward to 309 Letcher Avenue. The Science Building was constructed with modern materials and the two-story exterior stuccoed building references the tradition of Gothic Revival architecture at VMI.

There was a ceremony on 11 November 2013 to celebrate completion of the building's significant renovation at a cost of over $19 million. All the electrical and mechanical systems were replaced, and centralized utilities such as laboratory gases were installed to support lab work. The exterior of the building was also improved, with a revised facade bringing the architecture in line with other buildings on Post and all the windows were replaced. The space was tailor-made to fit the needs of the chemistry and biology departments housed there. The emphasis on labs related to both the chemistry and biology departments. The 62,408-square-foot Maury-Brooke Hall now includes 11 teaching labs, 14 research labs, 20 offices, five classrooms, a three-bay greenhouse, and study spaces for cadets.

The newly renovated Maury-Brooke Hall features an enlarged foyer that exhibits the rich history of scientific study at the Institute and features artwork honoring the two distinguished scientists and professors for whom the building is named. A larger than life plaster statue of Maury is situated prominently in the foyer. The seven-foot seated figure was given to VMI in 1929 by its creator, Frederick William Sievers, after it had served as the model for the bronze statue located on Richmond's Monument Avenue.

Also, a painting depicting the battle of the ironclad vessels USS Monitor and CSS Virginia hangs in the foyer. The scene illustrates one of the many accomplishments of Brooke, who was a primary designer of the Confederate ironclad CSS Virginia vessel. In addition to these works of art, two plaques are installed in the foyer featuring images of Maury and Brooke along with brief biographies.

Other features of the foyer include a display case that contains historical artifacts associated with the chemistry and biology departments, illustrating the development of these fields of study. Images of current scientific study at VMI are displayed on a large monitor in the foyer, linking current cadet and faculty research with the past.

Matthew Fontaine Maury

Matthew Fontaine Maury was an American astronomer, historian, oceanographer, meteorologist, cartographer, and geologist. He was born on 14 January 1806 in Spotsylvania County, Virginia, near Fredericksburg. When he was five years old, his family moved to Franklin, Tennessee. He wanted to follow in the footsteps of his older brother who had been a Flag Lieutenant in the United States Navy. Thus, he joined the Navy in 1825, at age 19, and became a midshipman on the frigate *"Brandywine"*, wanting to learn quickly all about the sea. Disappointment due to the lack of education from the ship's instructor quenched his hopes, but he did study the seas and record methods of navigation.

His next assignment on the sloop *"Vincennes"* provided the same frustrations. But Maury pursued self-education as the ship did have a library. In spare moments on duty, he chalked problems in spherical geometry on cannon balls stored on deck. In the summer of 1830, he was able to gain immense practical experience in spherical geometry, as the *"Vincennes"* returned to New York having circumnavigated the globe. He developed an interest in writing books and articles about the oceans. He published his first book in 1830, titled *"Navigation after a Voyage around the World"*. In 1836 he published a second book called *"A New Theoretical and Practical Treatise on Navigation"*.

In 1839, Maury expanded his study of navigation, meteorology, winds, and currents, and he was appointed the superintendent of the Navy's Depot of Charts and Instruments in 1842. Two years later the department was renamed the United States Naval Observatory.   Maury's primary duties were to care for the U.S. Navy's chronometers, charts, and other navigation equipment. He had access to thousands of ships' logs and charts from all over the world, and he used this material to compile and interpret data about winds and currents. In 1847, he published the *"Wind and Current Charts of the North Atlantic"*. It showed sailors how to use the ocean's currents and winds to significantly shorten the length of their ocean voyages. A few years later in 1851 he published *"Explanations and Sailing Directions to Accompany the Wind and Current Charts"*. This work provided material for his more famous book, *"The Physical Geography of the Sea"*, which was published in 1855, and credited as the first textbook of modern oceanography. Maury's uniform system of recording oceanographic data was used by navy ships and sailors around the world. It was also used to develop charts for all of the major ocean trade routes of the time. In fact, he bested Great Britain's admiralty in securing the fastest, safest routes to India and Australia, and helped connect America and Europe with the first transatlantic telegraph cable.

The American Civil War broke out in 1861 and, on 20 April 1861, Maury resigned from the United States Navy three days after Virginia seceded from the Union. Since he was born in Virginia, he supported the Southern Cause and joined the Confederacy as the Chief of Sea Coast, River, and Harbor Defenses. During the war, he was sent to England to acquire warships and supplies for the Confederate Government. He also worked on defending the harbors and invented an electrical mine to be used against enemy ships. He also pleaded with other nations to intervene and help stop the Civil War. After the war ended, Maury led a Confederate immigration to Mexico, where Emperor Maximilian helped establish a colony of Virginians.

Maury later went to England after Maximilian was defeated. He stayed there until 1868, when he returned to the United States to become a professor of meteorology at the Virginia Military Institute. Maury lectured to cadets on occasion. One of his principal jobs was to write a physical survey of the state of Virginia, and the cadets helped with that work gathering field samples, drawing maps, and helping in other ways. Near the end of his life, Maury labored to establish a national weather service to do for farmers and merchants what he had done for shippers and mariners. It was his last unfinished crusade.   In 1872, he became ill while conducting an exhaustive lecture tour. He died on 1 February 1873 at the age of 67, and was temporarily buried in Lexington. His body was then moved to Hollywood Cemetery in Richmond, Virginia, where it remains today.

In spite of his involvement in the Civil War, the United States forgave him. Maury Hall was named in his honor at the U. S. Naval Academy in Annapolis and at VMI. The VMI Gilham House was renamed in honor for Maury in 2010. He received honors from many parts of the world, including being knighted by several nations. Many monuments have been created to honor him, and he even has a crater named for him on the Moon. His important contributions to the fields of oceanography and ocean navigation have earned him many titles, including "Pathfinder of the Seas" and the "Father of Modern Oceanography".

John Mercer Brooke

John Mercer Brooke was also an American sailor, engineer, scientist, and educator. He was instrumental in the creation of the transatlantic telegraph cable, and was a noted marine and military innovator. John Mercer Brooke was born at Tampa Bay, Florida, on 18 December 1826, the son of an Army officer, General George Mercer Brooke. He became a U.S. Navy Midshipman in 1841, graduated from the U.S. Naval Academy in 1847, and achieved the rank of Lieutenant in 1855. His Navy career was marked by sea duty and scientific assignments.

While stationed at the U.S. Naval Observatory in Washington, D.C., during the early 1850s, he worked with Commander Matthew Fontaine Maury charting the stars as well as assisting in taking soundings of the ocean's bottom to determine the shape of the sea floor. Many believed the sea floor was flat, but all previous soundings as deep as eleven miles could not find the ocean bottom. Part of this was due to powerful undercurrents far below, and rivers in the ocean traveling in various directions. In the struggles with soundings, which nobody had done anything of value at great depths, it was Maury's unique device he invented that gave Brooke an idea of taking deep sea soundings. Brooke perfected a deep-sea sounding device which was used afterwards by navies of the world until modern times and modern equipment replaced it. At Maury's direction, Brooke also added a core-sampling device for taking samples of the material of the sea floor.

Brooke also took part in surveying and exploring expeditions in the Pacific during the middle and later parts of the decade, and helped instruct officers of the inexperienced Japanese Navy. He had a role in the counseling and instruction of officers of the nascent Japanese Navy. In Japan, he was a technical adviser aboard the Japanese steamer *"Kanrin Maru"* and he helped sail the ship to the United States in February 1860.

Following the secession of Virginia from the Union, Brooke resigned his Naval commission along with Matthew Maury in April 1861 and "went south" joining the Confederate Navy as a Lieutenant. He was deeply involved in the conversion of the frigate *"USS Merrimack"*, designing the armor for the ironclad *"CSS Virginia"*. He also had charge of the Confederate experiments for the development of the torpedo for submarine boats. In 1862, he was promoted to Commander and, in 1863, to Chief of the Confederate Navy's Bureau of Ordnance and Hydrography until the end of the war. He was instrumental in the design and production of heavy rifled 7-inch guns for the Southern war effort produced at the Tredegar Iron Works in Richmond, Virginia, and the Confederate Naval Ordnance Works at Selma, Alabama. A new rifled gun for the Confederate Navy became known as the Brooke rifle. He was also instrumental in the organization and establishment of the Confederate States Naval Academy.

After the Civil War, on 9 October 1865, Brooke, of the prewar U.S. Navy and of the Confederate States Navy, was named to a new chair of Physics and Astronomy at the Virginia Military Institute, which embraced astronomy, physical geography, and meteorology. He was a professor at VMI from 1866-1899, while continuing his technological pursuits and had a regular teaching load very involved in the cadets' day-to-day academic life. In 1891, Francis Mallory, class of 1889, came to learn physics under John Brooke, and Mallory was later Brooke's successor as head of the Physics Department.

After a long career of teaching, he retired to his home built in 1875 at 501 Brooke Lane on Diamond Hill in Lexington until his death on 14 December 1906. He is buried in the Stonewall Jackson Memorial Cemetery. The US Navy honored Brooke's career by naming the first ship of a new class of Destroyer Escort/Fast Frigate ships in his name - USS BROOKE. It was the lead ship of guided missile frigates in the United States Navy from 1962-1988.

I.19. William L. Moody, Jr. 1886 Hall

Moody Hall is located west of the Parade Ground at the corner of Letcher Avenue and VMI Parade street. The building was completed in 1971 for the VMI Alumni Association, on the site of the former Anderson House, which had served as the VMI Alumni House from 1934 until it  was demolished in 1968. The building was named for William Lewis Moody, Jr., a VMI cadet in the Class of 1886 and a Texas businessman. On 25 January 1965, Mrs. Mary Moody Northen from Galveston, Texas, the daughter of William Moody, donated $800,000 to VMI to build a new building.

The new alumni building is sited slightly to the west of the former Anderson House, allowing the road around the Parade Ground to curve as originally envisioned in the Goodhue plan. The two-story limestone building has a one-story Tudor-arched porch across its Parade Ground façade. Moody Hall, sometimes happily called the Moody Hilton, was dedicated in October

1969 by Senator Harry F. Byrd, Jr. Its completion was made possible by Mrs. Northen's further generosity in the amount of $203,000, 25% over the original estimate.

On the side facing the Parade Ground are two flights of steps up to the porch from the sidewalk. The one on the left leads to the entrance lobby. A spacious lounge lies inside the entrance lobby and to the left is the Moody Library containing memorabilia of the Moody family and providing ample room for a group meeting. Inside right of the entrance lobby is a large room for multiple activities, including large meals. The first floor also contains the usual restrooms, cloak rooms, and a kitchen. In the back of the building is the office for the Alumni Foundation and on the second floor is a dormitory for 50 Alumni.

William Lewis Moody, Jr.

William Moody was born in Fairfield, Texas on 25 January 1865, and passed away in Galveston, Texas on 21 July 1954. At the age of nine, it is recorded that he was sent to Roanoke, Virginia, to attend Hollins Institute. After attending two other boarding schools in Virginia, he went to VMI for two years and, in 1884–85, he and his brother Frank went to Germany to further their education. After returning home, Moody briefly studied law at the University of Texas before joining his father's firm on his twenty-first birthday in 1886. He became a significant financier, entrepreneur, and philanthropist.

After a brief stay in New York as the representative of the W. L. Moody and Company, he closed the New York office and returned to Galveston. Moody persuaded his father in 1889 to open a bank in Galveston, which became the W. L. Moody Bank. Upon his father's death in 1920, he became president of the W. L. Moody and Company, Bankers, the W. L. Moody Cotton Company, and the American National Insurance Company. After 1920, he established the American Printing Company of Galveston, the National Hotel Corporation, and purchased the *Galveston News* and the *Galveston Tribune*. He also owned eleven ranches in Texas and Oklahoma, and enjoyed them for duck hunting and fishing, as well as raising cattle, sheep, and goats.

Moody served one term in 1921–23 as treasurer of the city of Galveston. He also was a colonel in the Texas National Guard. Moody's legacy to the people of Texas was the Moody Foundation of Galveston, established by Moody and his wife in 1942. The foundation focused on a small number of projects, including the Moody State School for Cerebral Palsied Children, before Moody's death. When the estate was transferred to the foundation on 29 December 1959, the foundation became one of the largest in the United States. It continues to be a major force in health, historical preservation, and education.

Mary Moody Northen

Mary Elizabeth Moody was the daughter of William Moody, Jr. and born in Galveston, Texas on 10 February 1892. She passed away in the same city on 25 August 1986. She married Edwin Northen in Galveston on 1 December 1915. The Northens had no children and enjoyed travel, ranch life, and community service. Edwin Northen died of a heart attack on 30 May 1954, and seven weeks later Mary's father died at age eighty-nine.

Mary Moody Northen became president and board chairman for all the Moody family enterprises on her father's death. She also chaired the Moody Foundation, founded by her parents in 1942. In 1964, Mary Moody Northen established the Mary Moody Northen Endowment as a charitable foundation which awards grants to support environmental, social service, educational, and historical projects benefitting people and institutions in Virginia and Texas.

Her personal interests included subsidizing many of the historical activities in Galveston, projects that often qualified for funds from the foundation. Her personal money and influence provided some unusual Galveston institutions. In addition to the funds donated to VMI and Hollins College in 1965, she commissioned *Lone Star*, an outdoor historical drama, and gave money to build a suitable theater in Galveston State Park. She purchased the abandoned Santa Fe Railroad depot and office building, and turned it into a railroad museum. She helped Texas A&M University form the Maritime Academy on Pelican Island in Galveston County. She gave funds to the Galveston Historical Foundation to secure the 1877 iron sailing bark *Elissa*, with a new figurehead for the vessel with Northen's face made from a picture in 1911. She lived in her family's home in Galveston until her death on 25 August 1986. The bulk of her $30 million estate was willed to the Mary Moody Northen Endowment to renovate and maintain the Moody home as a historic museum.

I.20. F. H. Smith Hall

F. H. Smith Hall is located at the west end of the Parade Ground, and lies between Moody Hall and the George C. Marshall Research Library and Museum. It was built in 1964 for the first VMI administrative building and named for the first VMI Superintendent Francis H. Smith. Smith Hall is a

two-and-one-half story stucco building with octagonal turrets on both sides of the entrance and crenellated parapet walls. The building also includes numerous window panes and a wooden entrance door.

Until 1964, the VMI administrative offices were included in barracks and other buildings. Now, most of the administrative offices are located in Smith Hall for the following provisions:

1. Superintendent's Office   2. Board of Visitors   3. Chief of Staff   4. Dean of the Faculty
5. Finance, Administration and Support   6. Procurement Services   7. Web Services
8. Communications & Marketing   9. Student Accounting

The Institute's first academic building, named Francis H. Smith Academic Hall, was constructed in 1900. It was a three-story brick classroom building within the U-shaped Old Barracks lacking a north side, and sited between the first Jackson Memorial Hall and the eastern side of Barracks. The building featured a central square clock tower with a crenellated parapet. Designed by local Lexington architect William G. McDowell, the building was named in honor of VMI's first Superintendent.

Based on the proposal by the new VMI architect Goodhue to finish Old Barracks as designed by A. J. West, Smith Hall was demolished in 1923 to add the north side of Old Barracks. To complete Old Barracks, it was also necessary to demolish the 1896 Jackson Memorial Hall.

Francis Henney Smith

Major General Francis Henney Smith was born in Norfolk, Virginia on 18 October 1812. An 1833 graduate of West Point, he married Sarah Henderson on 9 June 1835 at West Point, New York, and they had seven children. Smith served as a second lieutenant in the U.S. Army until he resigned his commission on 1 May 1836 and moved to Hampden-Sydney College, Virginia as professor of mathematics, about 30 miles east of Lynchburg, Virginia.

In 1839, the VMI Board of Visitors considered two candidates to be the head of the new Institute. One of the Board of Visitors members was John T. L. Preston, who successfully

recruited Smith. Preston was a graduate of Washington College and, by the time classes had begun on 11 November 1839, he was appointed to the faculty and worked with Smith at VMI until retiring in 1882.

Francis Smith was unanimously selected as the VMI Superintendent by the Board of Visitors, and the other candidate was Joseph Reid Anderson. Also a West Pointer, Anderson had graduated in 1836, joined the U.S. Army, but resigned in 1837 to work as a civil engineer with Virginia State Engineer Claudius Crozet, who had earlier been a professor of engineering at West Point. Anderson was born in Fincastle, Virginia, owned the Tredegar Iron Company that provided most of the ammunition in the Civil War, was a Brigadier General in the Confederate Army, and was the uncle of William Alexander Anderson whose house was purchased in 1934 to be the VMI Alumni House.

As head of the newly established Virginia Military Institute, Smith served for fifty years, from the Institute's infancy, through the Civil War, and through the difficult post-war period. He is known as the "builder and rebuilder of VMI." Smith retired on 1 January 1890 and died only a few months later on 21 March 1890 at his house on Diamond Hill in Lexington, Virginia, next to John Brooke. He was buried in the Stonewall Jackson Memorial Cemetery in Lexington.

By 1840, the outmoded arsenal quarters and his expectation for a growing cadet population spurred Superintendent Smith into an expansion campaign. His initial effort added three new buildings near the original Lexington Arsenal. The first completed was his home, a three-story brick building close to west of barracks and facing south. A two-story mess hall was constructed at a location southeast and down the hill from the Lexington Arsenal on the same general site as today's Crozet Hall. The third new building was reconstructed next to the north side of the militia barracks.

Supportive of expanding construction at VMI, Smith connected with Philip St. George Cocke, who was a wealthy Virginia planter, West Point graduate, and member of the VMI Board of Visitors since 1846. Cocke felt there was a need for a beautiful and inspiring plan for the new Institute, and was determined to see VMI become the great polytechnic institute of the South and renowned for its distinctive architecture. Cocke was an advocate of the Gothic Revival style and had employed the nationally prominent architect Alexander Jackson Davis to design his villa, known as Belmead, in Powhatan County, Virginia. During a visit to Cocke's residence circa 1848, VMI Superintendent Smith and John T.L. Preston were impressed by Davis' work and subsequently influenced VMI to hire Davis to design the new barracks building.

Davis wrote to Superintendent Smith that "...a building of such extent and combining so many uses will require invention to bring it within a modest appropriation". Smith responded that the barracks would include a chemistry laboratory, lecture rooms, debating rooms, and a library. Davis' idea was for a rectangle barracks building four stories high with rooms opening upon "stoops" inside the barracks. The rooms were planned to accommodate three cadets and to be about 20 x 16 feet rectangular. The object included plans for rooms to accommodate 200 cadets entirely disconnected from each other and one arched entry on the south side of barracks (the Washington Arch). In March 1850, the Virginia legislature concurred and provided $46,000 for construction, and John Jordan, builder of the Lexington Arsenal, was contracted to construct the Old Barracks building under Superintendent Smith's supervision.

In February 1856, Congressman John Letcher brought the name of Colonel Smith to the attention of the U. S. Secretary of War and his endorsement resulted in Smith's appointment as member of the Board of Visitors of the Federal Military Academy. As president of this board, Colonel Smith, who was superintendent of the largest state military institution, was closely associated with a former West Point classmate who was serving as superintendent of the Federal Military Academy.

In addition to his focus on new buildings for the Institute, in 1858, Colonel Smith took a trip to Europe to look at institutions with a scientific and military character. Smith ultimately desired to adopt the system he considered the L'École Polytechnique in France as the greatest of the military technical schools where Claudius Crozet attended. Also while in Europe, Smith purchased a sword for the son of General Richardson, who described his son as being the best cavalry officer in the Virginia.

Smith was the author of *An Elementary Treatise on Algebra* (1858) and co-author of *The American Statistical Arithmetic, Designed for Academies and Schools* (1845), *Best Methods of Conducting Common Schools* (1849) and *College Reform* (1850) and translator of *An Elementary Treatise on Analytical Geometry* (1860). In 1859, he sent a report to the General Assembly of Virginia recommending that VMI be organized as a general scientific school, with three special schools of application: one agriculture; two, engineering; and three, fine arts. The Civil War interrupted this project, but the modifications were ultimately made.

At the outbreak of the Civil War, Smith was appointed a Brevet Brigadier General in the Virginia Militia on 24 April 1861, then a colonel in the 9th Virginia Infantry Regiment on 7 July 1861. He was often absent, returned to VMI when it reopened in late 1861, and was appointed "Major General of Cadets" on 18 December 1861. He was dropped as colonel of the 9th Virginia Infantry Regiment in the reorganization on 8 May 1862. On 11 June 1864, Major General David Hunter, who had replaced Sigel after the New Market battle, ordered a retaliatory attack with his troops burning and shelling VMI's campus.

Smith oversaw the reconstruction of VMI after its destruction. As a result of the Reconstruction Act in March 1867, Virginia became Military District number one. At that time, a new state legislature came into being. The majority of the legislature was hostile and did not look kindly on the VMI. The committee adopted a resolution in 1868 ordering Smith to show why VMI should not be obliterated. The superintendent, a great persuader, with political finesse as well as vigor, rose to the occasion. He convinced the lawgivers of VMI's great potential through its technical know-how to aid the restoration of the life and economy of Virginia. General Smith gained the tacit support of the first commander of Military District number one, Major General

John M. Schofield. A key point in gaining legislative reversal of the hostility events by its committees resolution was the information that the celebrated scientist Matthew Fontaine Maury was about to join the Institute faculty and would conduct the physical survey of the state, including railroads and other transportation routes, soils, and minerals. His physical survey of Virginia was of tremendous value to the state, and it cost VMI $20,000, which was never repaid.

Unrelated to Smith's "builder and rebuilder of VMI", he participated in more elements for VMI. For example, the motto of VMI, the one which appears on its seal, was first mentioned by Superintendent Smith in a letter written to General Richardson on 20 November 1841. Smith said: "I have been thinking of the design of the cadet flag. I should have a representation of the coat of arms of Virginia on one side and on the other a simple figure of Minerva with the emblems of war and in her hand a flag with the motto: '*Virginiae fidem praesto.*' I am true to the Old Dominion, may be the English of it." The motto was "*Faithful to Virginia*". This expression was often referred to as VMI's motto during the period 1841-1875, however, it was never officially adopted.

On 28 June 1876, Superintendent Smith recommended to the Board of Visitors another motto, "*In Pace Decus, In Bello Praesidium*", translated "*In Peace a Glorious Asset, In War a Tower of Strength*". This motto of the Institute was adopted by the Board of Visitors on 28 June 1876, and reaffirmed by the Board in 1969. Smith is also known as the Sigma Nu International Fraternity's spiritual founder and he was on the VMI Board of Visitors from 1884 to 1887.

I.21. Marshall Hall – Center for Leadership and Ethics

Marshall Hall, located west of the Parade Ground behind Smith Hall and the George C. Marshall Research Library and Museum, is named for General George Catlett Marshall, Jr., a VMI graduate in the class of 1901. Construction of the building was completed in 2008 dedicated as Marshall Hall on 1 May 2009. It is also named the Center for Leadership and Ethics based on the performance and accomplishments of General Marshall. Although its architecture does not include the Gothic Revival style, it does feature colored stucco walls, similar to other VMI buildings.

The building includes significant rooms and offices. Left of the center entrance is a very large conference room, two stories high, used for meetings, banquets, conferences and a variety of VMI events including the annual Ring Figure Ball. The second story above this room is a balcony open to the first floor, and is used primarily for banquet meals. The walls surrounding the balcony present the VMI Hall of Valor with pictures and military medals of VMI graduates who participated in various military wars.

To the right of the main entrance is the 500-seat Gillis Theatre, named for Leslie Gillis, Jr., VMI class of 1929. He received a law degree from George Washington University and followed a legal career until he changed to be a real estate operator. The theater has routine facilities and equipment, including two dressing rooms; light-sound doors, enabling late arrivals to enter without disturbing other spectators; a large rehearsal-storage room; an off-stage video room enabling performers to follow the play's progress while off-stage; and dual stages that can be divided to accommodate multiple settings. Joellen Bland, who worked at the theatre since 1978, and became its director in 1982, stated: "Truly, this new theater is a long-awaited dream come to life."

George Catlett Marshall, Jr.

Marshall was born on 31 December 1880 in Uniontown, Pennsylvania and died on 16 October 1959 in Washington, D.C. He is buried in the Arlington National Cemetery. A member of the VMI class of 1901, he was the top ranking VMI cadet as First Captain, played tackle on the VMI football team, and was initiated into the Kappa Alpha Order after his graduation. Supporting VMI, Marshall served on the VMI Board of Visitors from 1946 to 1954. His career included 44 years in the U.S. Army, when he was promoted to a 5-star general as General of the Army, U. S. Secretary of State, and U.S. Secretary of Defense.

"The Marshall Affair" is an interesting short story in the 1901 yearbook "Bomb" that included numerous Marshalls at VMI. Richard Marshall was the Commandant and ordered St. Julien Marshall, the Officer of the Day guard, to report cadets yelling from their window in barracks. When George Marshall yelled from the window in Harry Marshall's room, the guard sentinel Myron Marshall heard and reported the yell, and Harry Marshall was given five demerits.

Following graduation from VMI, at 20 years old, George Marshall served briefly as the commandant of students at the Danville Military Academy in Danville, Virginia, because the Reserve Officer Training Corps program was not established until 1916 and Marshall had to pass an exam to achieve his commission as a second lieutenant of infantry in the U.S. Army. He passed the exam and was appointed to the U.S Army in February 1902. He then married Elizabeth (Lily) Carter Coles on 11 February 1902 at her mother's home, the Pendleton-Coles House, which is now the VMI Admissions Office at 307 Letcher Avenue.

Marshall had an extensive life as an American soldier and statesman, which echoes the VMI theme of "citizen-soldier". He rose through the U.S. Army from 1902-45, serving ultimately as the U.S. Army Chief of Staff under presidents Franklin D. Roosevelt and Harry S. Truman during World War II. Winston Churchill lauded Marshall as the "organizer of victory" for his leadership of the Allied victory in World War II. After his military service, Marshall was appointed by President Truman as Secretary of State from 1947 to 1949, and advocated a significant U.S. economic and political commitment to the post-war European recovery, which was named the Marshall Plan. He also served as U.S. Secretary of Defense from 1950 to 1951 under Truman as a result of the Korean War which began on 25 June 1950.

Soon after he received his Army lieutenant appointment, he was sent to participate in the Philippine-American War in May 1902, first as a platoon leader and later a company commander. After its defeat in the Spanish-American War of 1898, Spain ceded its longstanding colony of the Philippines to the United States in the Treaty of Paris. The Philippine-American War began in 1899 when the Muslim people who lived in the Southern Philippines wanted their independence. Although a peace treaty for the "Moro War" was signed on 2 July 1902, battle continued between the Filipino guerrillas and the U.S. Army until 1913, and Marshall remained in the Philippines until November 1903. After returning to the U.S., Marshall participated in numerous assignments from engineering officer to infantry, and attended several military schools before returning to the Philippines in June 1913 after the "Moro War" ended. He was there with the 13th Infantry as Chief of Staff of Field Detachment 1 and later served as aide-de-camp to Brigadier General Hunter Liggett to prepare plans for defense of the Philippines.

Marshall returned to the United States in 1916 to serve as aide-de-camp to the commander of the Army Western Department, Major General James Franklin Bell, at the Presidio in San Francisco. General Bell had served as Chief of Staff of the United States Army from 1906 to 1910. Marshall relocated with Bell to Governors Island, New York when Bell was reassigned as commander of the Department of the East and assumed responsibility for Officers' Training Camps in New York at Plattsburgh, Madison Barracks near Sackets Harbor, and Fort Niagara. George Marshall was directly involved in the logistical support for these camps, battling a sluggish army supply system to properly equip the volunteer citizen soldiers. In August 1917, these camps graduated the largest quota of new officers needed for the new National Army, as World War I had begun in July 1914.

Major General John Joseph Pershing was also at Governors Island until May 1917, when he was selected as Commander of the American Expeditionary Force after the United States declared war on Germany in April 1917. That summer, Marshall became chief of staff for operations of the 1st Division managing the mobilization of the 1st Division for service in France. Overseeing the division's mobilization and organization in Texas, he departed for France arriving on 26 June 1917.

Marshall served with the 1st Division on the St. Mihiel, Picardy, and Cantigny battle fronts. He won recognition and acclaim for his planning of the attack for the Battle of Cantigny, in May 1918, for the first notable American victory of the war. In mid-1918, he was posted to the headquarters of the American Expeditionary Force, where he worked closely with General Pershing, and was a key planner of American operations. He was instrumental in the planning and coordination of the Meuse-Argonne Offensive, which contributed to the defeat of the German Army on the Western Front in 1918. During the Great War, Marshall had multiple roles as a planner of both training and operations. Marshall held the permanent rank of captain and the temporary rank of colonel; he was recommended for promotion to temporary brigadier general in October 1918, but the Armistice occurred on 11 November 1918 before the promotion resulted. After the war, Marshall reverted to his permanent rank of captain.

After WWI, General John Pershing became Chief of the U. S. Army in May 1919, stationed in Washington, D. C., and Marshall was selected as his aide-de-camp from May 1919 to July 1924, promoted to major in July 1920 and lieutenant colonel in August 1923. Marshall worked in a number of positions for the army, focusing on training and teaching modern, mechanized warfare. After this period, Marshall was assigned the commanding officer of the 15th Infantry in Tientsin, China.

Several nations were providing military personnel in Tientsin for its protection and safety. Tientsin was a large city significant for its support to trading Chinese products around the world, and located between the capital Beijing and the shipping ports on the Bohai Bay. At that time, the situation in China was like civil war with large armies led by numerous warlords. Marshall developed close interaction with the Chinese during these incidents, which gave him keen insight about the Chinese forces fighting each other, and the character of Chinese soldiers and their relationship with the Chinese population. This experience gave Marshall insight into the extent of military and political influence of foreign countries and foreigners in China. When Marshall departed China in May 1927, Chiang Kai-shek, was working to develop diplomatic relations between the nation's population and working to defeat the warlords fighting for control of Beijing. This civil war continued for twenty years, and Marshall was sent to China again after World War II as a diplomat to create peace and patience in China.

Returning to the U.S. after China, Marshall worked as an instructor at the Army War College, assistant commandant of the Infantry School at Fort Benning, Georgia, commanding officer of the 8th Infantry at Fort Screven, Georgia, and was promoted to colonel in September 1933. From 1933 to 1936, he was a senior instructor for the Illinois National Guard in Chicago, Illinois. Marshall was promoted to brigadier general in 1936 and commanded the 5th Brigade of the 3rd Infantry Division and Vancouver Barracks in Vancouver, Washington from 1936 to 1938. During this period, he also was responsible for 35 Civilian Conservation Corps (CCC) camps in Oregon and southern Washington. The CCC was a public work relief program as a part of Franklin Roosevelt's "New Deal" that operated from 1933 to 1942 for unemployed and unmarried men, and Marshall initiated a series of measures to improve the morale of the participants and to make the experience beneficial in their later life.

In July 1938, Marshall returned to Washington, D.C. and was assigned to the War Plans Division on the War Department staff, becoming the Army's Deputy Chief of Staff. Attending a conference in the White House at which President Roosevelt proposed a plan to provide aircraft to England in support of the war effort, and Marshall was the only person to voice disagreement based on required logistical support or and training. All the attendees voiced support of the plan except Marshall, who was impressed by President Roosevelt.

After the Army Chief of Staff Malin Craig retired on 1 September 1939, the same day the German Army launched its invasion of Poland, Marshall was nominated above many higher generals by President Roosevelt to be the Army Chief of Staff due to his career and high intelligence, and he was promoted to a 4-star general. On December 16, 1944, Marshall became the first Army general promoted to the five-star rank, and was entitled the General of the Army. He was the second American to be promoted to a five-star rank, as William Leahy was promoted to Fleet Admiral the previous day. The five-star rank was also termed field marshal, and created by Congress. Marshall held this position until his retirement on 18 November 1945 after WWII ended.

As General of the Army, Marshall organized the largest military expansion in U.S. history, inheriting an outmoded, poorly equipped army of 189,000 men. He coordinated the large-scale expansion and modernization of the U.S. Army, in part by picking or recommending many of the Army generals who were given top commands during the war including Dwight D. Eisenhower, George S. Patton, and Omar Bradley. Both Eisenhower and Bradley attended the dedication of the Marshall Research-Museum at VMI in 1965.

Faced with the necessity of turning former civilians into a force of over eight million soldiers by 1942, Marshall approved an abbreviated training schedule for men entering the Army. At the time, most U.S. commanders at lower levels had little or no combat experience of any kind. In consequence, Army forces deploying to Africa in Operation Torch suffered serious initial reverses when encountering German armored combat units in Africa at Kasserine Pass and other major battles. Even as late as 1944, U.S. soldiers undergoing stateside training in preparation for deployment against German forces in Europe were not being trained in combat procedures and tactics.

During World War II, Marshall was instrumental in preparing the U.S. Army and Army Air Forces for the invasion of Europe. He wrote the document that would become the central strategy for all Allied operations in Europe. He initially scheduled Operation Overlord for 1 April 1943, but it was delated until 6 June 1944 due to strong opposition from Winston Churchill, who convinced Roosevelt to commit troops to Operation *Husky* for the invasion of Italy.

It was assumed that Marshall would become the Supreme Commander of Operation *Overlord*, but Roosevelt selected Dwight Eisenhower as Supreme Commander. While Marshall enjoyed considerable success in working with Congress and President Franklin D. Roosevelt, he refused to lobby for the position. President Roosevelt didn't want to lose Marshall's presence in the states. He told Marshall, "I didn't feel I could sleep at ease if you were out of Washington.

Throughout the remainder of World War II, Marshall coordinated Allied operations in Europe and the Pacific. He was characterized as the organizer of Allied victory by Winston Churchill. In addition to accolades from Churchill and other Allied leaders, *TIME* magazine named Marshall its "Man of the Year" for 1943. Marshall retired from active service in 1945, but remained on active duty, as regulations required continued duty for holders of five-star rank. When his military career ended, Marshall took on a diplomatic career. He had key diplomacy experience during WWII, participating with presidents Roosevelt and Truman in conferences for the Atlantic Charter (1941-1942), Casablanca (1943), Quebec (1943), Cairo-Teheran (1943), Yalta (1945), Potsdam (1945), and in many others.

On 15 December 1945, Marshall traveled to China serving as a special envoy to negotiate a coalition government between the Nationalists under Chiang Kai-shek and Communists under Mao Tse-Tung. Marshall was able to work with both sides but, eventually he concluded there was no way to make a peaceful cooperation, returning to Washington, D.C. in January 1947. Two years later in 1949, Chiang Kai-shek and his Nationalists were required to move to Taiwan Island east of China. Marshall was awarded the United States Congressional Gold Medal in 1946, the highest civilian award in the United States, which also included General John Pershing.

On 21 January 1947, President Truman appointed Marshall the Secretary of State. The prior Secretary James F. Byrnes had worked at developing treaties between the U.S. and countries that supported the recovery of Germany and Austria. In addition, there were significant internal problems in Turkey and Greece due in part to outside Communist pressures by Russia.

In March 1947, Marshall attended a conference in Moscow with ministers of Britain, France and Russia to discuss European boundaries, economic recoveries, government structure, and other elements. Lacking any agreements, primarily due to the Russian minister Molotov, Marshall requested and conducted conversation with the dictator of Russia, Joseph Stalin. Unfortunately, there were no agreements in that meeting either. After returning to the U.S., Marshall worked with his deputy Dean Acheson and created a staff in the Department of State to focus on a plan for recovering the European economy. On 5 June 1947, Marshall was invited to receive an honorary degree at Harvard University, and presented in his speech the outline for a European Recovery Plan.

For the second time, in 1947, Marshall was named "Man of the Year" in the TIME magazine. He was honored again due to his principal purpose for rebuilding Europe and modernizing its economy, a program that became known as for the Marshall Plan. Working with President

Truman, both sides of Congress, and major leaders in Britain and France, the European Recovery Program was authorized by Congress and signed by Truman in April 1948. The plan for the European recovery was to extend for four years with $12 billion approved by Congress. In recognition of his work to revive Europe, Marshall was awarded the Nobel Peace Prize in 1953.

Marshall resigned from the State Department because of ill health in January 1949, but in the same month became chairman of the American Battle Monuments Commission. In September 1949, he was selected as the president of the American National Red Cross and left that position in September 1950 when President Truman appointed him to be the Secretary of Defense. Marshall was selected as Secretary of Defense because the Korean War had started on 25 June 1950 and Truman trusted Marshall to restore confidence and morale for the military while rebuilding the armed forces for combat in Korea. Marshall also worked to rebuild the difficult relationship between the Defense and State Departments, as well as the relationship between the Secretary of Defense and the Joint Chiefs of Staff.

The appointment required a congressional waiver for Marshall because the National Security Act of 1947 prohibited a uniformed military officer from serving in that post. This prohibition included Marshall because individuals promoted to General of the Army are not technically retired, but remain officially on active duty even after their active service has concluded. General Marshall was the first person to be granted such a waiver. The second military general appointed to Secretary of Defense in January 2017 was Marine Corps General James Mattis.

The division of Korea between north and south followed World War II, after Japan's 35-year rule over Korea ended. In 1945, Korea north of the 38th parallel was occupied by Russia and Korea south of the 38th parallel was occupied by the United States. Negotiations between U.S. and Russia failed to reunify Korea, and the Korean War started in June 1950 when North Korean armed forces invaded South Korea. Within several months, strong North Korean forces had defeated 90 percent of South Korea.

Fortunately, General Douglas MacArthur landed approximately 75,000 U.S. soldiers in Inchon, Korea, just west of Seoul, and close to the 38th parallel in September 1950. These forces pushed southward behind the North Koreans and defeated so many of them that the surviving North Korean forces moved back north across the 38th parallel on 1 October 1950. The South Korean forces continued to push north above the 38th parallel and, a week later, having received authorization from Marshall, MacArthur proceeded to conduct operations in North Korea. As a result, the Republic of China unleashed a counter-attack in October 1950 pushing the line of war back south to the 38th parallel.

Following Chinese military intervention in the Korean War, Marshall and the Joint Chiefs of Staff sought ways to aid MacArthur while avoiding all-out war with China. In the debate over what to do about China's increased involvement, Marshall opposed a cease–fire on the grounds that would make the U.S. look weak in China's eyes. In addition, Marshall argued that the U.S. had a moral obligation to honor its commitment to South Korea. Marshall opposed diplomatic overtures to China, arguing that it was impossible to negotiate with the Communist government. In addition, Marshall expressed concern that concessions to China would undermine confidence in the U.S. among its Asian allies, including Japan and the Philippines. When some in Congress favored expanding the war in Korea and confronting China, Marshall argued against a wider war in Korea.

In mid-1951, negotiations began to restore North and South Korea, and Marshall chose to retire as Secretary of Defense on 12 September 1951, at the age of 72. After resigning, Marshall retired to his home in Leesburg, Virginia to tend to his gardens and continue his passion for horseback riding. This was his first and only permanent residence owned by Marshall who later said "this is home...a real home after years of wandering." He was an American statesman and soldier consistent with the VMI contemplated role of citizen-soldier. Fighting continued near the 38th parallel, dividing Korea until the Korean Armistice Agreement was signed 27 July 1953.

Marshall had been on the VMI Board of Visitors from 1946 to 1954, and was also president of the VMI Foundation Board in 1949 and 1950. When Marshall Arch was dedicated on 15 May 1951, General Marshall attended and was awarded the Virginia Distinguished Service Medal.

In a television interview after leaving office in 1952, Harry S. Truman was asked which American he thought had made the greatest contribution over the preceding thirty years. Without hesitation, Truman picked Marshall, stating "I don't think in this age in which I have lived, that there has been a man who has been a greater administrator or a man with knowledge of military affairs equal to General Marshall." Marshall was also head of the American delegation at the coronation of Queen Elizabeth II in 1953.

Marshall died at Walter Reed Hospital in Washington, D.C. on 16 October 1959 at the age of 78. He received a Special Military Funeral after lying at the Washington National Cathedral for 21 hours, guarded by representatives from all the U.S. armed services, as well as a VMI cadet. President Dwight D. Eisenhower ordered flags flown at half-mast, and was among the invited guests at the funeral service at the Fort Myer Old Post Chapel. Other dignitaries at the funeral included former President Truman, former Secretary of State Dean G. Acheson, Generals Omar N. Bradley and Matthew B. Ridgway. Following a 19-gun salute, Marshall was buried at Arlington National Cemetery in Arlington, Virginia, in a place he had picked beside his first wife, Elizabeth Carter Coles (1875–1927) and her mother Elizabeth Pendleton Coles (1849–1929), and his second wife, Katherine Tupper Brown Marshall (1882–1978).

I. 22. George C. Marshall Research Library and Museum

The Marshall Research Library and Museum is located on the west end of the Parade Ground, on the north side of Smith Hall. Owned by the Marshall Foundation, it is a memorial to General George Catlett Marshall, Jr., a 1901 VMI graduate. He was a member of the U. S. Army for 43 years, serving as Chief of Staff and General of the Army, and later the U.S. Secretary of State and U.S. Secretary of Defense.

Completed in 1964, the one-story cinderblock building has stone detailing similar to Marshall Hall. Its architecture does not reflect the Gothic Revival style, but its colored stucco matches other VMI buildings. The picture taken at the dedication of the George C. Marshall Library and Museum on 23 May 1964, includes left to right former president Dwight D. Eisenhower, President Lyndon Johnson, and General Omar Bradley.

The Library has collected, preserved, and made available documents of the life and public service career of General Marshall. The material includes a variety of related military and diplomatic history about Marshall between 1900 and 1960. He was born on 31 December 1880 in Uniontown, Pennsylvania, and died on 16 October 1959 in Washington, D.C.

The library is composed of twelve groups based on Marshall's assignments and the offices he held, including Fort Benning, 1932; Fort Screven, 1932-1933; Fort Moultrie, 1933; Illinois National Guard, 1933-1936; Vancouver Barracks, 1936-1938; Pentagon Office (includes deputy Chief of Staff and Chief of Staff period), 1938-1945; China Mission, 1945-1947; Secretary of

State, 1947-1948; American Battle Monuments Commission, 1949-1950; American Red Cross, 1949-1950; Secretary of Defense, 1950-1952; and Retirement, 1951-1960.

Each subgroup includes biographical material; correspondence; shorthand notebooks; speeches; statements and writings; engagement books; and scrapbooks. The online digital collection also includes six annotated volumes published by the Johns Hopkins University Press.

A large "talking map" dominates the west wall in the World War II museum wing. The map was designed by the National Geographic Society, and the text was provided by Forrest C. Pogue, Marshall's biographer. In addition to the introductory video, there are three main spaces in the museum.

The main lobby addresses Marshall's early years in Uniontown, Pennsylvania and at VMI, and his Army service before and during World War I. The "Organizer of Victory" exhibit in the west wing focuses on General Marshall's military leadership, including his many innovations and contributions to winning World War II. The "Soldier of Peace" exhibit in the east wing focuses on Marshall's role after World War II as Secretary of State, promoting the European Recovery Program, and his role as Secretary of Defense during the Korean War. The Nobel Peace Prize he received in 1953 for his contributions to restoring the European economy through the Marshall Plan is on display in the Marshall Museum.

Nobel Peace Prize

See the I.21. Marshall Hall article for the biography of General Marshall.

Section II. VMI Houses

VMI houses are very historical and contribute significantly to the VMI Historical District. The VMI Post has historic residences that reflect a variety of architectural styles from Neoclassical to Gothic Revival and Italianate. The oldest house now on the VMI Post is a residence built in 1818 by and for John Jordan, who was the builder of the Lexington Arsenal in 1816 that became the Virginia Military Institute in 1839, and was contracted to do the stone work for the construction starting VMI Old Barracks in 1850. Another historical house was built in 1850 by John Jordan's son Samuel, a residence located behind Crozet Hall, which was converted later to the VMI Post Hospital.

Some houses built over 150 years ago have been demolished. One was built in 1840 next to the southwest corner of the former Virginia Arsenal barracks as the first residence for Superintendent Smith. It was built on a narrow strip of land purchased from Samuel Moore next to barracks. Another house was built on the southeast corner of barracks in 1845 as a residence for Thomas Williamson, the third faculty member. Both houses were demolished in 1851 to make space for construction of the present Old Barracks that started in 1850. Another house was built in 1843 by Samuel Moore on his property, which would now be close to Moody Hall and the southwest end of the Parade Ground. It was purchased by VMI in 1908, and demolished in 1953. Another house was built for Superintendent Smith in 1847, further west of barracks, and was demolished in 1860, when a decision was made to build a new and recent Superintendent's Quarters. Smith moved into the Moore house until the new Superintendent's Quarters was built in 1862.

New houses were built for Thomas Williamson and William Gilham in 1852 at a location which was between the north and south of the Parade Ground and just east of the "Old Guard" tree. Both of these houses and the Superintendent's Quarters were designed by the first architect at VMI, A. J. Davis and moved from the center of the Parade Ground north to the edge of Woods Valley in 1914 in order to expand the Parade Ground. This movement was an object of Bertram Goodhue, the second best VMI architect. The Williamson House was demolished in 1965 to construct Lejeune Hall, which was demolished in 2006 to construct the Third Barracks. The Porter's Lodge, built in 1852 for overnight guests and faculty, was also at the southwest end of the Parade Ground, east of Moore's house, and was demolished in 1912 to extend the Parade Ground.

Much more information will be provided in this section about the houses mentioned above and others that are very historic on the north side of the Parade Ground, Letcher Avenue, Institute Hill, and Diamond Hill. The VMI houses contribute to the VMI Historic District which was listed in the National Register as a National Historic Landmark in 1975.

The portrait below was painted in 1857 by Casimir Bohn (1816-1883), and shows from left to right the Moore House, Porter's Lodge, Superintendent's Quarters, the Gilham and Williamson houses, Old Barracks, the Old Hospital and the mess hall. Bohn was a native of Germany and best known for publishing books of engravings of Washington, DC, which were among the most popular ever made. He also published photographs of engravings of the University of Virginia and other places as well as the Virginia Military Institute.

II.A.1. "Jordan's Point"/"Stono"/Turman House

The Turman House built in 1818 is the oldest house on the VMI Post and is located east of Crozet Hall at the end of Stono Lane. Stono Lane was the historic estate's carriage drive and today is the street for the buildings along this ridgeline. Constructed by John Jordan for his residence in 1818 with his partner Samuel Darst, the residence was called "Jordan's Point" because of the owner's name and its location on the bluff overlooking Jordan's Point where Jordan's family had important business and transportation operations next

to the North River, which is now called the Maury River. The house was renamed "Stono" by the Jordan family in 1930.

The Locher family purchased "Stono" from the Jordans in 1958, and sold it to the VMI Foundation in 1986, after a significant donation to the VMI Foundation by Solon Turman and his wife Dolly. In 1993, the VMI Foundation renamed "Stono" the "Turman House" and, in 2005, the house was transferred from the VMI Foundation to VMI property. "Stono" was listed on the National Register of Historic Places in 1975 and included in the Lexington Historic District. The Turman House is now a contributing historical building to the VMI Historic District.

This stately brick residence is one of the earliest Neoclassical style buildings west of the Blue Ridge Mountains, and one of Virginia's earliest examples of Roman Revival architecture. The front walk, approximately eight-feet wide, is dry-laid brick in a herringbone pattern. There are three more buildings on the property -- a "summer kitchen" behind the main house, an ice house where ice from the Maury River was stored, and an office to the east that was likely built for Jordan's slaves. The property also had a pond that was used to hold fish caught in the river.

The Turman House sits on a limestone foundation. and has an overall T-shape with the broadest façade facing east, which overlooks the Maury River. The front façade of the Turman House faces south and can be seen in the picture as a two-story, three-bay wide and three-bay deep center section, flanking one-story wings, and a gallery at the second-floor level. Each of the wings is two-bays wide, and the entire house, except for the portico, is encircled by a four-course, molded-brick cornice. The original windows have six-over-six glass panes placed in double-hung wood frames, with modern aluminum sashes set outside the original wood frames and louvered shutters are located at each window opening.

Jordan's colossal Roman Doric portico came from the classical Palladian architectural scheme of the ancient Greeks and Romans. This portico was recalled from his work in 1806 when he was remodeling Thomas Jefferson's Monticello and his work at the University of Virginia in 1817. The four Tuscan columns support the triangular gable, which has a metal-framed fanlight over the central entry.

The main entrance has a six-panel wood door encircled with a notched cornice and a similar door opens onto the second floor from the portico. The large entry hall on the first floor leads south to a library, north to the dining room, and west to a stair hall which climbs to two bedrooms. Beyond the stair hall is a living room. The central hall, library, living room, and second floor bedrooms have plaster walls and ceilings with wood paneling on the lower part of the walls. The fireplace mantel in the entrance hall has columns with small rounded moldings and with elliptical sunbursts carved over them. The floors have random width pine boards.

The library fireplace has an iron stove made by Jordan himself at his ironworks. Enclosing the firebox is cast iron with circular and elliptical surrounding panels. Chimneys rise at the north and south facades and the fireplaces retain cast iron inserts with fine engaged columns on either side of the opening. Another chimney was constructed and stands at the west façade.

The original mantel in the library has thin columns surmounted by wooden blocks with carved vertical, elliptical sunbursts on three sides. Wood paneling on the lower part of the walls, topped by a chair rail, decorates the library. The woodwork in the dining room and parlor resembles the library, but with minor differences of detail such as the use of paneled wood rather than rounded moldings in the parlor mantel.

The central stair hall has an elegant stair. The stair banister has rectangular uprights and a handrail at the side of the staircase, and a thin newel post at the top and bottom of the stairs with curious detail. The banister passes over the newel and terminates in a delicately carved dog's head on the handrail which is said to represent Jordan's favorite hound. The original flooring in the stair hall has been replaced with a parquet floor.

The kitchen at the back of the Main House is accessed through both the north dining room and the west living room. The kitchen has preserved the bulls-eye moldings at doors and windows, but has been updated with new appliances, cabinets, and linoleum flooring. To the rear of the south wing, a one-story porch forms an L where it extends across the one-story wing and the Main House. The porch roof is supported by circular brick columns formed with specially molded bricks.

Additions were made periodically to the Turman House. About 1870, a one-and-a-half-story rear wing was added connecting the main house to a formerly separate weaving house, extended 60 feet to the rear (south). At some point prior to 1883, a two-story, two-bay deep addition was added to the west end of the main house. A two-story brick addition was constructed at the west end of the center section prior to 1883, expanding it by two-bays. At the west side of the north wing a one-story, shed-roofed addition was altered and to the rear of the west façade, a gabled addition was constructed. Two other rooms have been added to the rear of the west wing. The exterior and interior of the Main House was restored in the 1980s.

The exterior of Turman House has good integrity and the interior is in excellent condition. On the interior, the overall floor plan has been preserved since the period 1883, and many historical finishes remain.

OFFICE

The Office is a one-room, one-story building with a full basement south of the Main house. The building is constructed on a local limestone foundation primarily of brick with a stone basement on the rear, downslope side. The low seam metal roof is pyramidal.

An internal brick chimney is located at the southeast corner of the roof. The main entrance is located on the north façade with a porch and the secondary entrance is at the basement level on the south façade, shown in the picture. Windows are modern six-over-six glass panes in double hung wood frames. The first floor windows have louvered shutters.

The Office has good exterior integrity, which has been altered with the installation of modern window sash and the interior has been renovated as a small apartment with modern finishes.

ICE HOUSE

The Ice House stands north of the Main House. The one-room building is constructed of stone on local limestone with a brick cornice under the edge of the roof. The exterior was originally covered with stucco. The low pyramidal shaped roof is covered with wood shakes. A board door enters the Ice House on the south, and small wood windows are located on the east and west. The house is currently used for storage.

SUMMER KITCHEN

The Summer Kitchen is a one-story, one-room building located to the northwest of the Main House. Constructed of local limestone masonry, there is evidence that the building was originally covered with stucco. The roof is covered with seam metal. An internal brick chimney rises at the north end of the roof. The single entrance has a paneled wood door located on the east façade. Windows on the east and west facades have six-

over-six glass panes in double hung wood frames. The single room on the interior is finished with plain plaster walls and ceiling, with a wood floor. The fireplace has a Neoclassical styled wood surround. The Summer Kitchen has good integrity on both exterior and interior.

John Jordan

John Jordan was born on 2 June 1777 in Goochland County, Virginia, located near Richmond, and later lived in Halifax County. Shortly after marriage in the spring of 1802, John and Lucy Jordan moved to Lexington, Virginia. When Jordan arrived in Lexington, he worked as a brick mason between 1802 and the War of 1812 for Benjamin Darst, who was a local builder and brick maker, but died in 1821. Jordan gained interest in the building and brick-making business from Darst, as well as iron making from his father, who made cannon balls for the patriot cause during the American Revolution.

He helped construct a few buildings, including Monticello and a school for girls called the Ann Smith Academy that opened in 1807. Jordan and Darst may have become familiar with the Neoclassical style through the use of builders' manuals, such as Owen Biddle's *Young Carpenter's Assistant* (1805), as well as by a direct connection to the final renovation of Thomas Jefferson's Monticello (1769-1808). An 1805 letter from Jefferson to Jordan indicates that Jordan provided brick building services at   Monticello, and received first-hand experience of the Neoclassical style from his work at Monticello. This experience led to introduction of the Neoclassical style to Rockbridge County with their work at the residences of" Stono", the "Beaumont" residence for Samuel Darst in 1819, and "Washington Hall" (1824) at Washington and Lee University.

The Lexington Arsenal building, constructed in 1816, was one of their early commissions. The VMI Old Barracks was also significant work of John Jordan.   A.J. Davis, the Old Barracks architect, relied on local builders to affect his plans. John Jordan stared construction of Old Barracks in 1850 under the supervision of VMI's Superintendent Smith. Jordan also built a house close to "Stono" in 1850 as a wedding present for his son Samuel. The residence was used for medical services as early as 1870 when the Old Hospital stopped serving that function, and named the VMI Post Hospital in 1909.

When tensions began to arise with Great Britain before the 1812 War, Jordan decided to join the military. He began serving as a Lieutenant in Virginia's Fifth Regiment, and was highly recognized for his valor. However, Jordan became frustrated with the militia because of the maneuvers around Chesapeake Bay, so he resigned and returned to Lexington. Shortly after his return, Jordan purchased fourteen acres of land he named Jordan's Point, located between the North River (Maury) and Wood's Creek.

Jordan gradually built a flourishing industrial and construction empire with his large family and slaves which included an iron foundry and forge, grist and flour mills, cotton and woolen textile manufacturing, lumber and metal shops, brick kilns, making and repairing machines, and architectural and construction work. For fifty years, he dominated building construction in Lexington and was responsible for nearly every important building erected there during that period. Jordan's interest in the iron industry extended to six counties: Rockbridge, Bath, Amherst, Louisa, Allegheny, and Botetourt. Throughout his life, he owned and operated ten furnaces to manufacture iron, which became a significant part of his business.

In 1818, he completed on the bluff above Jordan's Point his large home, which is now owned by VMI as the Turman House. Jordan was also influential in developing the commercial economy in Lexington by promoting improvements in transportation. Jordan was a prominent contractor and road builder, and was aware of the need for better transportation within the Shenandoah Valley. Jordan built the road over North Mountain and helped improve the stretch between Covington and Lynchburg, by way of Lexington.

"The Point" had long been an important location for transportation in Rockbridge County, with a ford providing river crossing at this location as early as the 1740s. During the 1820s, he constructed the Balcony Falls section of the James River and Kanawha Canal. Their ownership was strengthened after the construction of a toll bridge in 1834.

Jordan also helped to improve navigation on the James River through construction of the North (Maury) River Canal, completed in 1851, which connected the North River to the James River and Kanawha Canal between Lynchburg and Richmond. Larger boats could navigate the James River through the Blue Ridge with much less trouble. The development of these transportation routes sustained the economic growth of Lexington until they were superseded by the railroad.

Jordan was president of the North River Navigation Company whose goal was to extend the canal to Jordan's Point. Major Thomas Williamson of VMI served as the engineer. The extension was not complete until 1860, after Jordan's death in 1854. The canal linked Lexington with markets to the east, making Lexington a trade center for counties to the north and west.

Jordan was also a member of the VMI Board of Visitors from 1846 to 1847. He died on 25 July 1854, at the age of 77, and was buried in what is now the Stonewall Jackson Memorial Cemetery.

Solon Brinton Turman, Jr.

Solon Brinton Turman, Jr., was born in Tampa, Florida on 2 March 1900. He was in the VMI 1920 Class, but left after his junior (2nd Class) year, and returned to Florida. Turman's mother was Matilda Lykes, whose father was Dr. Howard Tyson Lykes. Matilda was sister to the sons of Dr. Lykes who started a shipping business in Tampa, Florida in 1898, that led to a great career for Turman. The brothers used a 109-foot, 75 ton 3-masted schooner named *Doctor Lykes* after their father to ship cattle to Cuba as a replacement for herds which were wiped out in the Spanish–American War. Solon Turman, Jr., was a nephew of the seven Lykes Brothers who founded the massive shipping, cattle, citrus and insurance empire bearing their name.

After returning to Tampa in 1919, he began his apprenticeship with the Lykes company as a cattle tender aboard one of the Lykes ships running between Tampa and Cuba. In 1921, he went to New Orleans, and served as a special European representative for the Lykes shipping firm, living in Belgium, Holland, Germany and England. In 1922, the seven Lykes brothers created the Lykes Brothers Steamship Company and, during the 1920s, its ships began to range beyond the Gulf of Mexico and Caribbean. Offices were opened in Europe, and routes were extended to the Mediterranean and Far East, and Turman became a director in 1925.

For thirty-seven years, starting in 1935, Turman played an important role in the development of American Merchant Marines, which refers to United States civilian mariners. In the 1930s, Lykes acquired 52 ships from Dixie and Southern States Lines, giving them a fleet of 67 ships. After passage of the Merchant Marine Act of 1936, they committed themselves to the replacement of their fleet with modern freighters. Sixteen had been delivered by December 1941, when the US entered World War II. During the war, Lykes carried 60 million tons of cargo and operated a maximum of 125 cargo ships for the government, and 22 ships were lost along with 272 lives. Many of the Lykes ships were named for family members and, in World War II, one of the merchant ships was named *Solon Turman*. Unfortunately, it was destroyed in the Caribbean by a German U-Boat on 13 Jun 1942.

Turman served as executive vice president for the Lykes Brothers Steamship Company in 1943, the country's largest shipping company. During the postwar years, Lykes returned to commercial activity. By the 1950s, it had a fleet of 54 ships totaling 568,978 deadweight tons, and Turman was president from 1951 to 1962.   That fleet underwent a complete replacement between 1960 and 1973, when 41 new ships were built, and Turman was chairman and chief executive officer starting in 1962. By then, Lykes Steamship had become a subsidiary of Lykes Corporation.

He retired as the director and chairman of the executive committee of Lykes-Youngtown Corp. and Youngstown Sheet and Tube Company in 1972 after a 52-year career, and was chairman of the board of Lykes Brothers Inc., which was the family's overall holding firm for its varied financial interests.

Turman had also been a former director of the Illinois Central Railroad and the Hibernia National Bank in New Orleans. He was also former chairman of the executive committee of the Committee of American Steamship Lines.

Turman had received a number of awards and was a significant benefactor with his wife Dolly. In 1949, he received the French Medal of Commercial Merit and, in 1957, he was named Louisiana's first "Maritime Man of the Year" by the Propeller Club of New Orleans. In 1961, President John Kennedy presented to Turman in a White House ceremony the American Legion's Merchant Marine Achievement Award. He was named *Man of the South*" by the "Dixie" business magazine in 1968. Also, on VMI Founders Day on 12 November 1973, the VMI Foundation's "Distinguished Service Award" was presented to Solon Turman by General Lemuel S. Shepherd, Jr., a 1917 graduate of VMI and chairman of the board of the VMI Foundation for Turman's career success and recognition of his long years of service to VMI.

Turman and his wife Dolly Hardee were also significant benefactors. In 1985, Turman gave $2 million to St. Joseph's Hospital in Tampa for an outpatient services and education center that was named in his honor. It unites outpatient health programs and community professional health education services in one complex. Turman was also a long time benefactor of the Touro Infirmary in New Orleans. He and his wife established a $3 million endowment for patients unable to pay for major unexpected medical expenses. The hospital also named it the Dolly and Solon Turman Ambulatory Treatment Center in their honor.

After Dolly Hardee Turman died in August 1983, a $3.25 million gift was given to VMI through the VMI Foundation in 1985 from the estate of the prominent New Orleans wife of Solon Turman. With the contribution, Mrs. Turman requested VMI to include an oil portrait of her great uncle, William J. Hardee, who was author of the infantry tactical manual published in 1855 and used by both Union and Confederate armies. Hardee was born in Georgia in 1815, graduated from West Point in 1838, and was a Union Army major when the manual was published. When the Civil War started, Hardee joined the Confederate States Army, and became a Lieutenant General. The manual was delivered to VMI in April 1863.

Although the donation to VMI was unrestricted for use, the Institute set aside $250,000 of the gift to refurbish in Preston Library a "rare book room", which was named the "Dolly Hardee Turman Rare Book Room". The room was dedicated in memory of Mrs. Turman in May 1985 ceremonies that were attended by her husband and members of his VMI class. A collection of 15 items depicting the Turman House is included in the Preston Library, with exterior and interior views, some with family members.

An oil portrait of the late Mrs. Turman was presented to Preston Library in 1989 where it now hangs just outside the Dolly Turman Rare Book Room named in her honor. The painting was unveiled at a small reception held in the Dolly Turman Rare Book Room in 1989 on the eve of the VMI sesquicentennial weekend. The oil portrait was the work of artist Susie Vaughan Neikirk from photographs and memory of her longtime personal friend. The noted Lexington artist, who was best known as a landscape watercolorist, was the wife of Joseph D. Neikirk, VMI Class of 1932, who was retired VMI Foundation executive vice president.

Solon Turman, a native of Tampa, Florida, and a momentous employee of the Lykes Brothers shipping companies, died at the age of 90 in New Orleans, Louisiana on 9 October 1990. He was buried in the Lykes Family Cemetery in Brooksville, Hernando County, Florida.

II.A.2. 450 Stono Lane House

In 1903, VMI built a pair of Queen Anne style officers' quarters on both sides of the former Samuel Jordan home, which is now the VMI Post Hospital. Designed by William G. McDowell, the twin buildings housed the Post Surgeon at 446 Stono Lane and the Post Chaplain at 450 Stono Lane.

In 2004, the Queen Anne house between the VMI Post Hospital and Crozet Hall was razed to make room for the expansion of Crozet Hall. The home at 450 Stonoe Lane remains between the Turman House and the VMI Post Hospital, and is still the residence of the VMI Post Chaplain.

The residence is a brick structure on a local limestone foundation. The two-and-a-half-story Queen Anne residence is square with a rear one-and-a-half-story wing at the northeast corner. A one-story addition with a shed-roofed porch stands to the west of the wing.

At the southern front façade exists a one-story wood porch with wood spindles and center stairs. The main entrance is located past the stairs and across the center of the porch, and the wood door has a large plate glass window. Above the center of the porch is a gable with patterned wood shingles.

The house has roofs covered with slate and windows exist on the rooftop with an arched window in the gable on the roof in the front facade. The two-and-one-half story brick building features small wooden blocks under the edges of the roof and decorative brickwork at the four chimneys. The brick masonry has both red and white mortar. Windows in the walls are two-over-two glass panes in double hung wood windows.

The interior double rooms are located on the corridor from the central hall. The interior retains the original floor plan as well as historical finishes. The main staircase with spindle work railings still commands the main entrance hallway. Original strip wood flooring, baseboards, five-panel doors, and window and door trim remain. The fireplaces have delicate Queen Anne tile and carved wood surrounds. The mantelpieces have elegant columns and low-relief garland decoration.

The residence has excellent integrity on both the interior and exterior, and is a good example of the Queen Anne style expressed in brick with patterned wood shingles at the gable ends. The majority of the character-defining features have been retained that include original wood windows and doors, slate roofs, wood entrance porch, interior flooring, wood trim, and fireplace surrounds. The residence is a contributing resource to the VMI Historic District.

II.B. VMI Parade

Six historical houses are located north of the VMI Parade Ground, including the Superintendent's Quarters and five faculty residences, on a street named VMI Parade. Two houses were built in 1852 and the Superintendent's Quarters in 1860. These three houses were designed by A. J. Davis and had the Gothic Revival architectural theme he rendered for VMI. Three houses immediately west of the Superintendent's Quarters were designed by Bertram Goodhue, following the Davis architectural theme, and were built in 1915. A similar Gothic duplex dwelling was built in 1927 west of the three Goodhue houses. All quarters north of the VMI Parade Ground are listed as contributing to the VMI Historic District.

II.B.1. Williamson House (Absent) – 416 VMI Parade

The Williamson House, built in 1852, was first located approximately in the center of the old drill ground, between barracks and the "Old Guard" tree. It was moved in 1914 to the north side of the drill ground on the edge of the Woods Creek ravine, two houses east of the Superintendent's Quarters. The house was built for Major Thomas H. Williamson, the third VMI faculty member. His first residence was built adjacent to the southeast corner of the arsenal barracks in 1841 and demolished in 1851 because Old Barracks construction started in 1850. The picture of the 1852 Williamson House was taken in 1915.

A. J. Davis' design of the Williamson House marked a return to symmetry. It was a two-and-one-half story stuccoed building dominated by a central three-story square tower, with crenellated rooflines and diamond-paned windows. During Major General David Hunter's VMI Raid on 12 June 1864, Williamson's House was extensively burned and damaged. The interiors were gutted and the roofs, parapets, towers, and some walls had collapsed. When the house was re-built after the Civil War in 1869, Scott Shipp moved into the renovated house. Thomas Williamson moved into a new house built in 1867 west of the VMI Post and south of present Letcher Avenue, which was demolished in 1988 for the construction of Maury-Brooke Hall. The 1852 Williamson House was demolished in 1965 to make room for construction of Lejeune Hall, which was soon demolished for the construction of Third Barracks.

Thomas Hoomes Williamson

Williamson was born on 30 August 1813 in Richmond, Virginia, but grew up in Norfolk, Virginia. He died on 31 March 1888 in Lexington, Virginia at the age of 74, after retiring from VMI in 1887. He entered West Point in 1829, and was a roommate of Francis H. Smith, VMI's first superintendent. He graduated in 1833 and became an assistant in the Office of the U.S. Engineer and helped build the dry dock in the Norfolk Navy Yard.

In 1841, Williamson was recruited by Superintendent Smith and joined VMI as the third faculty member. He served as Professor of Engineering and Drawing until his retirement in 1887, two years before Smith retired. He was also a mathematics professor for Washington College students who could attend classes at VMI until 1847. (VMI cadets could also attend classes at Washington College.) Williamson was also the Commandant of Cadets from 1841 to 1845. In 1849, he was promoted to Major and wrote the textbook "*An Elementary Course in Architecture and Civil Engineering*" for use in his cadet classes. In 1855, he was appointed the VMI Librarian.

Williamson was also an engineer for John Jordan, president of the North River Navigation Company, whose goal was to extend the North River (now the Maury River) Canal starting at Jordan's Point and leading to the James River. It was completed in 1851. The North River Canal was finally connected to the Kanawha Canal in 1860, linking Lexington, Lynchburg and Richmond, and making Lexington a major trade center. With Williamson's support, development of these transportation routes sustained the economic growth of Lexington until they were superseded by the railroad.

Williamson had various special assignments during the Civil War. When the war started in April 1861, he was promoted to Lieutenant Colonel, served with the Confederate Corps of Engineers, and worked on the defenses of the Rappahannock River and Manassas. In October of that year, he was ordered to return to VMI to teach Civil and Military Engineering, but he was recalled to the Confederate Army in April 1862 for temporary special duty on the staff of General "Stonewall" Jackson. After the Civil War, he returned to VMI. At his retirement in 1887, he was promoted to Brigadier General.

II.B.2. Gilham/Maury House – 414 VMI Parade

The Gilham/Maury House is located on the VMI Parade street east of the Superintendent's Quarters. Along with the Williamson House, it was another VMI residence designed by A. J. Davis, and built in 1852 for William Gilham. The house has a two-story octagonal tower with a three-story square turret. It is another Gothic Revival faculty residence on the northern edge of the Parade Ground. The picture was taken in 1910.

The house is notable as the only asymmetrical building designed by Davis at VMI, despite the fact that Davis exclusively used asymmetry in most of his architecture. Like the Williamson House and the Superintendent's Quarters, this house was first located approximately in the center of the old drill ground, east of the "Old Guard" tree, and was moved in 1914 to the north side of the expanded Parade Ground. Like the Williamson House, the house was built for Major Gilham in 1852 because his former residence was demolished in 1851. That previous residence was built in 1841 for Smith on the southwest corner of the former Arsenal Barracks,

Gilham lived in the new house with his large family until it was badly damaged by the raid of General Hunter in 1864. After the attack, the Gilham House had no doors, windows or roof, the interior was gutted by fire, and the exterior masonry looked like it might have been shelled. After the war, Gilham moved to Richmond because there was no residence for his large family and no salary at VMI. The residence was repaired by 1868, and Matthew Fontaine Maury lived there and taught at VMI until 1873 when he died at the age of 67. The house was later inhabited by Commandants of Cadets, Deans, and VMI faculty. This residence was named the Gilham House until 2010 when additional renovations were made and it was renamed the Maury House.

In 1914, the house was carefully dismantled so the old drill ground east of Old Barracks could be expanded to be a parade ground. The house was reconstructed where it is now, over a basement using original house materials, but with new floors, new exterior stucco, bathrooms, and a rear kitchen addition. In 1956, electrical and plumbing systems were upgraded, and the building added new overhead light fixtures, bathrooms, and a kitchen. The entry was moved to the octagonal ground floor room, and the double-leaf, diamond-panel door was replaced. The former entry area was converted to a bathroom, and the signature octagonal room was changed from a living room to circulation space. Most significantly, the front porch was removed and deprived the house of a major character-defining feature.

The goal in 2010 was to restore the building's historic appearance – to respect the spirit of Davis' design – while again updating its electrical, plumbing, and HVAC systems. The result is a 21st-century residence, with modern conveniences carefully woven into the building's original fabric. A screened porch on the rear of the house was removed to make way for an addition that can be used as a family room. The 1956 bathroom was taken out, a double-leaf, diamond-panel door was put back, and the turret was returned to a sitting room. In addition to a period-appropriate interior paint scheme, the bathrooms in the house have a turn-of-the-century flair. Original moldings, window casings and fireplace mantels from the 1870s were preserved. The most significant part of the exterior restoration is the return of the front porch, which restores the house's scale, proportions, and silhouette as Davis intended.

William Henry Gilham

William Henry Gilham was born in Vincennes, Indiana, on 31 January 1818. His father's family was from Virginia. He was appointed to the United States Military Academy (now West Point) where he graduated 5th in the Class of 1840. After graduation, he became a lieutenant in the 3rd Artillery in the United States Army and fought in the Seminole War in Florida. From September 1841 to August 1844, he was Assistant Professor of Natural and Experimental Philosophy at the U.S. Military Academy. He also served in the Mexican-American War in 1846, and in the same year became the fourth faculty professor at VMI. He was also appointed Commandant of Cadets in 1846. When the Gilham family came to VMI, no quarters were
available for them and for a time they boarded with the steward in the mess hall. Gilham moved into the Superintendent's first house next to barracks in 1847 when Smith left for his new home half way to the Porter's Lodge.

Major Gilham taught in what is now the guard room in Old Barracks and his Commandant's Office was in Washington Arch. Over the next five years, he developed VMI's Departments of Physical Sciences (optics, astronomy, chemistry, mineralogy, and geology), taught infantry tactics, and served as the Commandant of Cadets. He also became Secretary of the VMI Academic Board.

To lighten the load on Major Gilham, VMI hired another professor in 1851, Major Thomas Jonathon Jackson, who was also a graduate of West Point, and a veteran of the conflicts in Florida and Mexico. Majors Gilham and Jackson taught infantry and artillery military training together at VMI for the rest of the decade. In November 1859, at the request of Virginia

Governor Henry A. Wise, Major Gilham led a contingent of the VMI Cadets Corps to Charles Town, seven miles west of Harper's Ferry, to provide an additional military presence at the hanging execution on 2 December 1859 of militant abolitionist John Brown following his raid on the Federal arsenal at Harper's Ferry. Major Jackson was placed in command of the artillery, consisting of two howitzers manned by 21 cadets. In response to the raid on Harper's Ferry, Governor Wise ordered Superintendent Smith to have Gilham write a manual to provide military training for volunteers and militia. Finished in the fall of 1860, it was 559 pages and titled *"Manual of Instruction for the Volunteers and Militia of the United States"*. It was initially published in Philadelphia, and was used by the U.S. Army for years.

As a professor, Gilham was very interested in geological matters. In 1857, his *"Report on the Soil of Powhatan County, Virginia"* was published in Richmond by Ritchie & Dunnavant. In the same year, he made a request to the Virginia legislature to fund acquisition of "a complete collection of minerals and fossils for the use of my classes", a copy of which is in the collection of the Virginia Historical Society in Richmond.

In 1861, as the American Civil War broke out, the Confederate Army had a lot of new recruits. Promoted to the rank of colonel, Gilham became the Commandant of Camp Lee in Richmond, Virginia, the camp of instruction for thousands of new confederate soldiers. When the VMI cadets arrived at Camp Lee in 1861 pursuant to the order of Adjutant General Richardson, it was the main reception and training center for Confederate recruits. Colonel Gilham was in command of the camp, as he had been relieved of his VMI duties. The VMI cadets were at Camp Lee to perform as drill instructors for the recruits. They followed Gilham's training manual, which was standard for both Union and Confederate armies. The cadets received plaudits from on high for their efficient job and they received much credit as their training led to success at the Civil War's First Bull Run Battle in July. Gilham's manual and the Corps of Cadets who were ordered to Camp Lee proved to be ideal training for the Confederate recruits.

Colonel Gilham briefly commanded a field brigade later in 1861 and 1862, but returned to teaching at VMI. On 15 May 1864, the VMI cadets participated in the Battle of New Market. Gilham was present, but did not command the young troops during the battle. After troops led by Union General David Hunter raided Lexington, and burned buildings at VMI including Gilham's house, the VMI cadets were stationed at Richmond for the remainder of the war. After the Civil War, VMI had no money to pay its instructors. As a result of no salary and no house for his large family, Gilham went to work and became president in Richmond for the Southern Fertilizer Company, which occupied the former Confederate Libby Prison facility near Richmond's Tobacco Row. One of the company's products, Gilham's Tobacco Fertilizer, was manufactured there. William Gilham died of undisclosed causes in Vermont on 16 November 1872, at the age of 54. He was interred in Lexington, Virginia's Stonewall Jackson Memorial Cemetery.

See the I.18. Maury-Brooke Hall article for the biography of Matthew Fountaine Maury.

.

II.B.3. Superintendent's Quarters – 412 VMI Parade

The Superintendent's Quarters is located on the north side of the Parade Ground within a row of faculty residences, and has served as the Superintendents' residence from its initial construction in 1860 to the present. This was the last VMI building designed by A. J. Davis.

The Superintendent's Quarters original location was approximately in the center of the old parade ground west of the "Old Guard" tree and the Williamson and Gilham Houses. All three houses were moved northward to the edge of Woods Creek Valley in 1914 as part of the architect Bertram Goodhue's plan to enlarge the parade ground. Though moved from its original location, the Superintendent's Quarters retained good exterior and interior integrity. The careful reconstruction preserved the patterns of the original building. Despite small alterations, the majority of the character-defining features have been retained. The original building had hipped roofs, but the current roofs are flat. The east and west chimneys were also removed. The interior has been altered with the installation of a second floor level in the main foyer, where the original building had a two-story entrance foyer.

The building is sited on sloping terrain and is two stories tall on the south side and three stories tall on the north. It is a symmetrical two-story stuccoed brick building with a central main entrance, semi-circular front porch, and twin octagonal turrets flanked by one-story wings. The semi-circular entrance porch forms an arc between the two turrets. Both turret and roof parapet walls are crenellated. The porch brackets have decorative scroll work with shield and axe patterns.

The main entrance is located at the center of the south façade under the porch. The double entrance doors form a triangular arch and are glazed with leaded, diamond-paned glass. Two additional entrances are located at the north façade, one at each wing. The east wing entrance is original and is designed in a similar style as the main entrance, with colored glass panes. The entrance at the west wing is a modern addition. The windows are diamond-paned, double-hung wood sashes, exhibiting several different patterns. Drip-mold crowns protect the windows and doors.

The interiors of the Superintendent's Quarters are also characteristic of Davis' work. Irregular stairways and arches are combined with octagonal spaces and Gothic Revival detailing at doors and fireplace surrounds.

The rear elevation features a semi-circular projecting porch that overlooks Woods Creek and was enclosed in 2003 at the request of Superintendent J. H. Binford Peay III. One former circular window at the north façade has been covered over and fitted with a decorative VMI logo grille.

This was not the first quarters for Smith. He actually lived first in the former Virginia Militia barracks beginning in 1839, when the Lexington Amory became the Virginia Military Institute. In December 1840, the VMI property was enlarged by a narrow strip bought from Samuel M. Moore adjacent to the west of former militia barracks and a house was erected on this lot for Smith in 1840. The picture drawn by Cadet

Charles Deyerle in 1842 shows the houses built on both sides of the Arsenal Barracks for Smith and Thomas Williamson. The Smith house was built where the southwest corner of Old Barracks now stands.

Superintendent Smith left his first house in 1847 after building another residence for himself further west of barracks, and sits left on the picture. VMI Headquarters also occupied this building. When Smith went to this new house in 1847, faculty member

William Gilham moved from barracks into Smith's first house. When Smith's 1847 house was demolished in 1860, in order to build the present Superintendent's Quarters constructed in the same spot, Smith was allowed to rent the Moore House, past VMI's small Porter's Lodge.

The present Superintendent's Quarters is closely associated with the first Superintendent, Francis H. Smith. Smith worked with A. J. Davis during the design of the early VMI buildings and oversaw the construction of Davis-designed barracks and officer's quarters. In the years leading up to the Civil War, Davis was anxious to complete what he named the "Executive Mansion" for Superintendent Smith. Its design completed the Davis concept for a group of Gothic Revival buildings like fortified enclosures with crenellation, towers, and turrets. When it was completed, Smith named the "Executive Mansion" the Superintendent's Quarters. From this residence, Smith guided the difficult rebuilding period for VMI following the Civil War and resided in the Superintendent's Quarters from 1860 until his retirement in 1889.

During Major General David Hunter's Raid on VMI on 12 June 1864, the Superintendent's residence was one of the few VMI Post buildings that escaped being destroyed. General Smith met with General Hunter, explaining that the child of his daughter was only 48 hours old, and that moving her might result in her death. As a result, the residence was spared and used by General Hunter as his headquarters, while Smith and his family moved to the Porter's Lodge. The Superintendent's Quarters was undamaged for these reasons, and did not suffer from fire damage like the majority of the other Post buildings.

II.B.4. Goodhue-designed Houses at 406, 408 and 410 VMI Parade

The three residences located at 406, 408, and 410 Parade Avenue, west of the Superintendent's Quarters, help line the northern edge of the Parade Ground. These three Gothic Revival residences were designed by Bertram Goodhue, the second best VMI architect, and constructed in 1915. From their original construction to the present, these buildings have served as faculty housing. The Gothic Revival quarters are architecturally significant as the quarters were designed to harmonize with the A. J. Davis Gothic Revival residences. They were constructed to provide officers' quarters. All three quarters are listed as contributing to the VMI Historic District.

Because all three houses were designed by Goodhue, it is no surprise that the houses have similar designs – interior and exterior. All three houses consist of a brick structure supported on a concrete foundation and finished with painted stucco. Houses 410 and 408 are two stories, while House 406 is two-and-a-half stories. They each have a turret that projects off the center of the south façade with a sun porch at the roof level and extensive window panes that are grouped.

Each house also has a main entrance with French doors located in the center of the south façade under a south, arcaded entrance porch. The first and second interior floors have rooms leading directly off a wide center hall. The interiors retain significant original finishes throughout, including stairwells, wood floors, wood trim, fireplace surrounds, and doors and door hardware. The kitchen and bathroom spaces have been renovated with new tile, cabinets, and finishes. The original floor plans remain intact, with two clear circulation paths for residents in the front and household staff in the back. On the back side, all three houses have a secondary entrance screened-in porch.

Houses 406 and 408 look similar on the south façade, except for the large porch openings with a flat-arched span at 408 and Gothic arches at the porch on 406. The Goodhue residence closest to the Superintendent's Quarters at 410 Parade Avenue has unique features, but also has features that match one of the other two houses. House 410 has three-bay wide, basket-handle arched arcade forms on the front entrance porch. The parapet walls along the south façade are slightly

crenellated with recessed square panel decorations. The rectangular turret that projects off the center of the south façade is beautiful with 120 window panes.

The front entrance porch at House 408 has one Gothic arched section and one flat-arched span with a horizontal stone beam bridging the opening. Another item of interest is a VMI plaque inset at the center of the south façade, above the arched section and under the crenellations on the parapet wall. Llike House 406, both have a one-story screened-in porch located at the northwest corner.

The front entrance of the 406 House is similar to the 410 House, with a three-bay wide, arched arcade entrance porch, but the arcades are Gothic rather than basket-handle arches. Houses 406 and 408 look similar on the south façade, except for the large porch openings with a flat-arched span at 408 and Gothic arches at the porch on 406. The turret at 406 is crenellated like the turret at 410 and atop the parapet at 408.

II.B.5. Duplex Quarters - 402/404 VMI Parade

The duplex dwelling at 402/404 Parade Avenue was constructed in 1927 and located along the north side of the Parade Ground at the most western end of the faculty residences row. This Gothic Revival duplex dwelling was designed in 1927 to harmonize with the adjacent Bertram Goodhue-designed residences. The site chosen for 402-404 Parade Avenue conforms with the arc of faculty residences and has been used as a residence since its initial construction

The rectangular, Gothic Revival residence is six bays wide and three bays deep. Supported on a concrete foundation, the exterior masonry walls are coated with colored stucco. The building has a flat, shed-style roof which slopes down towards the rear. Crenellated parapet walls crown the roofline. Windows are composed of single and grouped wood casement sash, which have interior screens. The window units consist of a twelve-paned casement sash below a fixed, six-pane transom.

Main entrances are located at the southeast and southwest corners. Each entrance has a nine-pane glazed wood door with a screen door. Main entrances are protected by a standing-seam, metal corner porch roof supported on decorative wood brackets. Secondary entrances are located at the north, rear elevation, giving access to the basements and first floors, through the screened-in porches.

The interior of 402-404 Parade Avenue has retained many of its character-defining features, including original fireplace surrounds, woodwork, built-in cabinets, and skylight. Minor interior renovations have been undertaken to modernize interior systems, with the greatest changes noted in the kitchens and bathrooms.

Both the interior and exterior of 402-404 Parade Avenue have good integrity. The original form of the residence has remained unchanged. Many character defining features are still extant and in good condition, including original wood casement windows, exterior glazed wood doors, and Gothic Revival entrance porches. On the interior, the original floor plan has been retained. Interior finishes, such as woodwork, fireplace surrounds, and wood floors have been maintained in good condition.

II.C. South Institute Hill and Diamond Hill

South Institute Hill area lies on the western end of VMI, and includes former historic residential buildings along and below Letcher Avenue. Several of the historic houses in this area have been demolished starting with the Moore-Pendleton-Bates House built in 1843, the Porter's Lodge, the Anderson House, and the house at 302 Letcher Avenue west of Neikirk Hall. Three other houses south of Letcher Avenue were demolished in 1988 in order to construct the new Maury-Brooke Hall. One of the houses was first owned in 1867 by VMI faculty member Thomas Williamson because his house was burned during the attack by the Union Army in 1864. The buildings remaining in this area all contribute to the VMI Historic District.

In 1874, the first street in this area was constructed and named "The Avenue". The new street started at the western VMI Limit Gates and crossed the Washington and Lee University (W&L) campus past the Lee Chapel westward to Main Street. It was the first street between VMI and W&L, and currently serves as the main entrance to VMI. In 1887, the Lexington Town Council formally renamed "The Avenue" the "Letcher Avenue" in honor of former Governor John Letcher. Letcher Avenue was extended from the western VMI Limit Gates eastward past Old Barracks to Main Street, and is now the main street through VMI.

In 1893, the picture to the right shows the original VMI Limits Gate that was designed by Thomas Williamson, the third VMI faculty member. These old gate posts are located on Letcher Avenue in front of Maury-Brooke Hall and mark the historic limits of VMI before its expansion west along Letcher Avenue after the Civil War. The gates identified VMI property line in 1857 and were known as the "1857 Limit Gates". Constructed of brick and inset with bronze

plaques, they were likely moved to their current location in the latter part of the nineteenth century after completion of Letcher Avenue in 1874. Historically, these supported metal gates controlled access to the Post.

Most of the houses in this area were constructed west of the original VMI Limits Gate by VMI members and Lexington residents as private residences between 1867 and 1900. Three houses were built on a trail before Avenue Street was completed in 1874. The buildings exhibit both wood cladding and brick masonry exteriors, with prominent front porches. The buildings are sited close together, reflecting a rural town setting. Diamond Hill, which is located south of Main Avenue beyond the VMI athletic facilities, includes twin Gothic Revival cottage residences constructed in 1875 and 1885, respectively, by VMI Professor John Brooke and VMI Superintendent Francis Smith. When the cottages were built, they were not on VMI property, but the cottages are now owned by VMI.

The first house built close to VMI was constructed in 1843 by Samuel McDowell Moore. First built on a horse trail, the address was later 310 Letcher Avenue before it was demolished in 1953. The first residential house for a VMI employee was built in 1867 by Dr. Robert Madison, the VMI Post Surgeon. It was first built where Maury-Brooke Hall now sits, but was moved to 309 Letcher Avenue in 1987. It was later named the Pendleton-Coles House, and is now the Admissions Office. An Italianate brick residence was also constructed in 1867 by a Lexington resident Samuel Moore, now known as the Cabell House at 306 Letcher Avenue. It is also stated that Thomas Williamson, another VMI faculty member, moved from his original house next to the Gilham/Maury House to south of Letcher Avenue in 1869. That may have been a house that was demolished in order to build the Maury-Brooke Hall in 1988.

In 1872, VMI faculty member Colonel William Blair built a brick Gothic Revival residence on The Avenue, which is now known as Neikirk Hall at 304 Letcher Avenue. In 1880, Samuel Letcher, son of the former Virginia Governor, John Letcher, constructed another Italianate brick residence at 305 Letcher Avenue. Also in 1880, former Governor John Letcher built a three-story vernacular wood-frame house for his two unmarried daughters located at 306 Main Street. It was acquired by VMI in 1945. The house formerly at 302 Letcher Avenue west of Neikirk Hall was built in 1907 by Greenlee Letcher and demolished in 1998.

Historical residences constructed on the south side of Letcher Avenue are now used for VMI Admissions Offices, the VMI Human Resource Office, VMI Protocol Office, and the VMI Police Department. The first house purchased by VMI was on the north side of Letcher Avenue at 304 in 1920, and at the same time VMI Post Limits were extended westward to Maiden Lane.

John Letcher (1813-1884) was a prominent attorney in Lexington, Virginia, a newspaper editor, Democratic Party leader in western Virginia, and a member of Congress in the 1850s. He led Virginia during the Civil War years and was best known as Virginia's Civil War-era governor, serving from 1860 through 1863. After the Civil War, he resumed his law practice and spent one session in the Virginia House of Delegates, 1875-1877. He was also an active member of the VMI Board of Visitors from 1867-1882, and served as its president for ten years. Letcher Avenue was named for him in 1887, and he had owned a lot of that property south of Letcher Avenue.

Below is a list of 9 houses on Letcher Avenue, with their locations, construction dates, original owners, the year purchased by VMI, and their present use. More information about all these houses, including the architecture, will be provided in this "VMI Houses" section.

Letcher Avenue Address	Constructed Date	Original Owner	Purchased by VMI	Use Now
301	c. 1875	May	1960	VMI Police Office
302	1907	Greenlee Letcher	1945	Demolished 1998
303	c. 1900	Letcher heirs	1981	VMI Protocol Office
304	1872	William Blair	1920	VMI Foundation Office
305	1880	Samuel Letcher	1956	VMI Human Resources
306	1867	Samuel Moore	1974	Faculty Residence
307	1894	Maria P. Duval	1945	VMI Admissions Office
308	1892	William Anderson	1934	Demolished 1968
309	1867	Robert Madison	1928	VMI Admissions Office

II.C.1. Moore-Pendleton-Bates House (Absent) - 310 Letcher Avenue

The Moore-Pendleton-Bates House was an historical house constructed in 1843 by Samuel McDowell Moore. The two-story Italianate brick residence had a prominent square cupola on the third floor. It was located past the west end of the Parade Ground and faced Lexington. The lot was at 310 Letcher Avenue in 1887. After it was purchased by VMI in 1908, the house became a residence for VMI faculty. The VMI residents in the former Moore House were Colonel Hunter Pendleton, a chemistry professor and, later, Colonel Robert L. Bates, head of the Physics and Science Departments. The house was demolished in 1953.

It is also notable than Moore was very involved with VMI Superintendent Smith. In December 1840, the VMI property was enlarged by a seven-acre strip bought from Samuel Moore adjacent to barracks, and a house was erected on this lot at the southwest corner of barracks for Superintendent Smith in 1841. More land was purchased from Moore later and another house was built for Smith in 1847, further west of barracks. When that house was demolished in 1860 due to construction for a new Superintendent's Quarters, Smith was allowed to rent the Moore House for two years – Smith's fourth dwelling location.

It is significant that Samuel Moore was instrumental in the site selection of the Lexington Arsenal that became the Virginia Military Institute. The location of the Lexington Arsenal was selected by a committee of five Lexington citizens appointed by Virginia Governor Wilson Cary Nicholas. Nicholas ordered the group to purchase approximately three-to-five acres of property for the arsenal. The committee was led by Samuel McDowell Moore and the committee selected a tract of five acres located on a high bluff above the North River, now the Maury River, where Old Barracks now stands.

Samuel McDowell Moore

Moore was born in Philadelphia on 9 February 1796, the son of Andrew Moore, who was an American lawyer and politician from Lexington, Virginia. Samuel Moore was a Washington College alumnus and studied law under George Wythe. He was admitted to the attorney bar in 1774 and rose to the rank of captain in the Continental Army during the American Revolutionary War. After the war, he was a delegate to the Virginia convention that ratified the United States Constitution in 1788. He represented Virginia in both the U. S. House and the U. S. Senate in 1789, and was a member of the Virginia legislature in 1791–1789 and 1799–1800. In 1803, he was commissioned a major general in the Virginia Militia. He served from 1825 to 1847 as a member of the Virginia House of Delegates, the Virginia Senate, and the U. S. House of Representatives, and then resumed his law profession. He served as a delegate to the secession convention in 1861 and, during the Civil War, served in the Confederate States Army. He died in Lexington, Virginia, on 17 September 1875, and was interred in the Lexington Cemetery.

II.C.2. Porter's Lodge (Absent) – West of Parade Ground

Porter's Lodge was the third VMI building designed by A. J. Davis and built in 1852 near the present southwest corner of the VMI Parade Ground and east of the Moore House. The picture shows Porter's Lodge was close to the original West Limit Gates and east of the Moore House.

The Lodge was a residence for the VMI porter, who was responsible for admitting and assisting those entering the VMI Post. It was a two-and-one-half story stuccoed building with symmetrical square turreted towers. Another Porter's Lodge was proposed, but never built, and the Moore House and the Porter's Lodge were torn down in 1912 due to Goodhue's plan to expand the Parade Ground.

During Hunter's Raid in 1864, the Porter's Lodge was one of the few VMI buildings spared because Superintendent Smith's daughter was sick with her new baby and was allowed to move with her parents from the Superintendent's Quarters into the Lodge. In 1866, five of the ten cadets who died from the Battle of New Market were rested in Porter's Lodge, and stayed until they were buried in the cadet cemetery in the spring of 1878.

After the Civil War, the Lodge was known as the "Tower" and housed VMI's art gallery which primarily contained portraits of VMI students. The portraits were transferred to the library in Old Barracks before the Lodge was enlarged in 1867 for use as a faculty residence for officers. The Lodge was then known as the "Round House" because of its architectural feature. The "Round House" residence included Colonel William D. Washington, who was head of the VMI School of Fine Arts inaugurated by Superintendent Smith in 1859. Washington was a significant artist and produced most of the portraits hung in the Tower's art gallery.

II.C.3. VMI Admissions Office (Pendleton-Coles House) - 309 Letcher Avenue

In 1867, Dr. Robert L. Madison, the VMI Post Surgeon, built a residence known today as the VMI Admissions Office, which sits at 309 Letcher Avenue. The house was built initially at the location of the present Maury-Brooke Hall, south of the trail that became The Avenue in 1874 and Letcher Avenue in 1887. The house was purchased by VMI in 1928. To provide space for Maury-Brooke Hall, the house was moved in July 1987 to its present location, outside the Limit

Gates. Earlier in the 1987 summer, four houses were razed in the area to provide a smooth path to move the house. It was a VMI faculty residence until it became used for the Admissions Office.

The two-and-a-half-story wood-frame house was known as a Gothic cottage, a design that was introduced into the Lexington community in the late 1840s, and continued through the 1850s and 1860s. The house is believed to be one of the first buildings completed in Lexington after the Civil War. It has a steep cross-gabled roof, board and batten siding, large bay windows, and decorative scrollwork "vergeboards" at the roof lines to hide the ends of rafters. The house had seven small coal-burning fireplaces, dumb-waiters built into the walls, and one of the first bathrooms in the VMI area - a very special treat for young ladies invited to stay there while attending Cadet Hops.

Dr. Robert L. Madison

Madison was the VMI Post Surgeon and professor of natural history from 1860 until his death in 1878. His grandfather was the youngest brother of President Madison. Dr. Madison accompanied the Corps of Cadets to New Market and remained with the wounded cadets when the battle was over. He was also physician to Generals Jackson and Lee, and to Commodore Matthew Fontaine Maury, who died in 1874. On his medical rounds at VMI, Dr. Madison's assistant drove a wagon drawn by a horse named "Gimlet". The horse and wagon suggested the term *"riding the Gim"*, which led the cadets to use "on the Gim" as an expression for being absent from duty with the doctor's permission. The house also served as an early meeting place of the Sigma Nu fraternity, founded by three VMI cadets in 1869.

Following Dr. Madison's death, his widow sold the house in 1881 to Colonel Edmund Pendleton, a member of VMI's first graduating class in 1842. The landscape at the Lexington Arsenal in 1839 was described by Pendleton, and he recalled that the old drill ground was partly under cultivation as a corn field and intersected by worm fences. He remembered the drill ground contained a few log buildings and a sole hickory tree, known as the "Guard Tree".

Pendleton had served in the Civil War, served as a member of the Virginia legislature, and was president of the VMI Alumni Association Board from 1868 to 1869 and a member of the VMI Board of Visitors from 1870 to 1873. The Pendleton-Coles House was named for Edmund Pendleton and his daughter Elizabeth, who married Walter Coles, and the house remained with his family for almost a half century. After Pendleton's death in 1899, the house was owned by his daughter, and it was in this house in 1902 that Pendleton's granddaughter, Elizabeth (Lily) Coles, married Second Lieutenant George C. Marshall, a 1901 VMI graduate. This house was purchased by VMI from Pendleton's daughter Elizabeth Coles in 1928, and

II.C.4. Anderson House (Absent) - 308 Letcher Avenue

The Anderson House no longer exists, but was located on the north side of Letcher Avenue (formerly 308 Letcher Avenue) and near the southwest corner of the Parade Ground where Moody Hall now sits. The house was built in 1892 for William Alexander Anderson. The three-and-a-half story brick, Queen Anne style house was acquired by VMI in 1934 from Anderson's heirs after Anderson died in 1930. The Anderson House was used as Alumni Hall from 1942 until it was torn down in 1968 to make room for construction of the new alumni building, Moody Hall. The

Anderson House was purchased by VMI primarily in order to convert a portion of northwest Old Barracks being used as alumni quarters and the Board of Visitors to create more cadet rooms that were required due to a higher enrollment. Fortunately, William H. Cocke was the superintendent when VMI purchased the Anderson House and was affluent enough to loan VMI the funds for the purchase.

Anderson was honored in the early 1960's when a street was constructed from the northwest corner of the Parade Ground down the Woods Creek valley and named Anderson Drive. This street on the North Post of VMI is a two-lane asphalt road that provides access to the Athletic/Physical Education Facilities and homes at the top of the north ridge past Woods Creek. The drive crosses Woods Creek via a 70-foot long two-lane bridge with concrete abutments and metal side rails. In general, the road and bridge are in good condition.

William Alexander Anderson

William Alexander Anderson was born on 11 May 1842, at Montrose, near Fincastle, Virginia in Botetourt County, the eldest of three sons and sixth of nine children of Francis Thomas Anderson, later a justice of the Virginia Supreme Court of Appeals, and Mary Ann Alexander Anderson.

He was educated at home and also attended the Fincastle Academy. Anderson enrolled at Washington College (later Washington and Lee University) in Lexington in 1857 but did not graduate. In April 1861 he left Washington College to join the Liberty Hall Volunteers, which he and his classmates had formed. He enlisted on 2 June 1861 and became orderly sergeant of Company I, 4th Virginia Infantry Regiment. Anderson was shot in the left kneecap at the First Battle of Manassas (Bull Run) on 21 July 1861, spent several months recuperating at the Richmond home of his uncle Joseph Reid Anderson, a prominent industrialist. He was discharged from the Confederate Army on 14 December 1861 and, in 1863, he entered the University of Virginia, where he received an LL.B degree on 20 June 1866.

While recovering from his kneecap injury in Richmond, William Anderson became a friend with his uncle's daughter Ellen Graham Anderson, and they were later married on 19 July 1871. Unfortunately, she died on 25 January 1872, only six months after they were married. Anderson later married Mary Louisa "Maza" Blair of Lexington, and they had four daughters and one son.

The Anderson House was not the only way in which Anderson helped VMI. Anderson returned to Lexington after graduation in 1866 and began a long and successful career as an attorney and important conservative Democratic politician. He was nominated to the Virginia House of Delegates in 1868 as a member of the Conservative Party, which sought to bring back the state's pre-war structure, but the state's military commander postponed the election. The next year, Anderson ran successfully for the Senate of Virginia and represented Alleghany, Bath, and Rockbridge counties from 1869 to 1873. In 1883, Anderson was elected to the House of Delegates from Rockbridge County as a member of the Democratic Party (the successor of the Conservative Party).

In the post-Civil War period, government funding was difficult. However, immediately in 1884, a budget request for VMI totaling $160,000 was presented to the Virginia General Assembly by the Honorable William A. Anderson. On 5 March 1884, Superintendent Francis H. Smith wrote a letter to his son stating: "The bill passed in the house by a vote of 57 to 23. My presence was necessary to aid and advise our delegates, but the whole credit for passing the bill is due to Anderson and Paxton (another Rockbridge County delegate). They watched our interest, and their bearing and vigilance did the work."

Anderson later joined the VMI Board of Visitors for one year from July 1886 to June 1887. In 1926, General E. W. Nichols, superintendent emeritus of VMI, referred to Anderson's service as follows: "William A. Anderson, now 84 years of age, has been practically coextensive with the life of the Institute."

Elected a trustee of Washington and Lee University in 1885, he served on the board until he died forty-five years later. Chosen president of the Virginia State Bar Association on 30 April 1900, Anderson also served for eight years as the Virginia Attorney General from 1 January 1902, until 1 January 1910. Anderson died at his house in Lexington on 21 June 1930, and was buried in Lexington, Virginia at the Stonewall Jackson Memorial Cemetery.

II.C.5. VMI Admissions Office - 307 Letcher Avenue

The building at 307 Letcher Avenue is located on the south side of Letcher Avenue between the VMI Admissions Office and the VMI Human Resources Office. Maria Duval was the original owner when the house was constructed in 1894. It was transferred to her half-sister Florence B. Duval in 1919 and purchased by VMI in 1945. After purchased by VMI, the house was used as a faculty residence until it changed to serve as offices for the VMI Director of Construction and, later, to be the VMI Protocol Office. It is now used as an annex to the Admissions Office. It is listed as a contributing historical building to the South Institute Hill area of the VMI Historic District.

The two-and-one-half story wood-frame residence at 307 Letcher Avenue was designed in a Queen Anne style architectural theme and has classical columns as porch supports. The wood-frame house was built on a local limestone foundation and is clad with horizontal wood siding. The duplex dwelling is square in plan with a projecting two-story bay window at the principal north façade. Measuring three-bays wide and deep, the house stands two-and-a-half stories tall on the north and three-stories on the south facing Main Street. The overall form, mass, and plan for this house have been retained, with preserved historical features such as interior woodwork, fireplace surrounds, and windows.

The cross-gabled roof is covered with standing seam metal roofing. The roof drains to a perimeter box gutter with downspouts at the building corners. Internal brick chimneys rise on the east and west sides of the roof. A three-story porch addition was added to the rear façade. The north façade has a prominent center gable, a two-story bay window on the east, and a one-story hipped-roof porch extending across the entire façade. The roof cornice has ornamental brackets. The two main entrances are located at the center of the north façade and have modern glazed doors and screen doors. Windows are typically two-over-two double-hung wood sash fitted with exterior screens. Also, Lexington Brick sidewalks, like the one in front of the house at 307 Letcher Avenue, are a character-defining feature on the Post.

On the interior, each side of the duplex dwelling has a hall plan with two rooms to the east and west. Modern finishes have been installed as part of the renovation for office space. However, some historical features have been retained including fireplace surrounds, original four-panel doors, and window and door trim with bull's eye moldings. All floors are now covered with wall-to-wall carpeting.

II.C.6. Cabell/Archer House - 306 Letcher Avenue

The Cabell House, located at 306 Letcher Avenue, was known earlier as the Archer House, and now sits behind Moody Hall. It was built in 1867 by Samuel McDowell Moore west of his first house built in 1843 on the trail between VMI and Washington & Lee that is now Letcher Avenue. The first recorded title, in October 1880, shows the property evolved to Mary E. Bruce. In 1894, a VMI civil engineering professor named Edward West Nichols purchased the home

and still owned it when he became VMI's third superintendent in 1907. Nichols moved into the Superintendent's Quarters, but retained the house until he sold it to Rose E. Archer in 1916, and she willed it to her daughters, Marie and Ellis. Marie died in 1968 and Ellis in 1972.

Purchased by VMI in 1974, the residence was renamed the "Cabell House" on 20 November 1976 due to funds provided by the Robert G. Cabell III and Maude Morgan Cabell Foundation for renovating the building and grounds. It was named primarily in honor of Robert Cabell's distant relative Cadet Sergeant William Henry Cabell, who died on the battlefield at New Market on 15 May 1864. His brother Robert G. Cabell, Jr., was also a VMI cadet who matriculated in 1863 and also fought in the Battle of New Market. Founded in 1957 by Robert G. Cabell, III, and his wife, the Cabell Foundation was established as a private, non-operating foundation to support the permanent needs of charitable organizations throughout Virginia, with particular emphasis on agencies in the metro Richmond region.

The house served as quarters for visiting guests and distinguished professors, and currently serves as a one-family residence for the VMI faculty. The residence at 306 Letcher Avenue is listed as a contributing historical building to the South Institute Hill area of the Virginia Military Institute Historic District. It is also a contributing building within the Lexington Historic District.

This Italianate brick residence at 306 Letcher Avenue is two-and-one-half stories tall, and is L-shaped with a rear ell addition. The main two-and-a-half-story block is three-bays wide and one-bay deep. The hipped roof is covered with standing seam metal roofing. The roof drains to hanging half-round gutters with downspouts at each building corner. Two internal brick chimneys rise through the center of the roof. The front-gabled rear ell is two-stories tall. The main south façade has a one-story, hipped-roof porch. Both the roof and porch cornices have simple bracket ornamentation.

The central main entrance has a four-panel wood door with three-light sidelights and a three-light transom. On the first floor, six-over-six double-hung wood windows reach down to floor level. The remaining windows are six-over-six double hung wood sash with louvered shutters and limestone sills. The interior has a center hall plan with a parlor and dining room located to each side. Rooms are finished with wood floors, original wood trim and doors, and marble fireplace surrounds. The central stair hall retains the gracefully curving stair. The rear ell is finished with simpler woodwork and fireplace surround details.

Renovations to the building included exterior as well as interior repairs. On the outside there were new roofs on all wings, front and rear porches were replaced, and repairs were made to all brick and woodwork. Inside, all the floors, walls and ceilings were either refurbished or replaced, new bathrooms were installed, and plumbing and wiring systems were completely replaced.

II.C.7. VMI Human Resources Office (Letcher House) - 305 Letcher Avenue

The house at 305 Letcher Avenue is now used as the VMI Human Resources Office, and is located between the Annex Admissions Office and the VMI Protocol Office. In 1880, Samuel Houston Letcher built the Italianate brick residence on "The Avenue", which is now 305 Letcher Avenue. When Sam died in 1914, ownership of the house was transferred to his brother Greenlee Davidson Letcher. After Greenlee died in 1954, the Letcher House was purchased by VMI in 1956. The building is listed as a contributing historical resource to the Virginia Military Institute Historic District.

After its purchase by VMI in 1956, it was used as faculty quarters and later converted to the Human Resources Office. The Italianate brick residence is two-stories tall with scrollwork decoration and a decorative bracketed cornice. The building is basically square in plan with a wood frame addition at the rear, south façade. Measuring two-bays wide and deep, the building is two-stories tall on the north and three-stories tall on the south. The low-pitched hipped roof is covered with standing seam metal roofing. The roof drains to hanging gutters with downspouts at building corners. An external brick chimney stands along the east façade.

The main north façade has a slightly projecting western bay. The roof cornice is decorated with a dentil course and paired modillions. An ornamental gable-end panel has a scrollwork pattern at its center. A one-story, hipped-roof porch extends across the entire façade. The porch has a simplified bracketed cornice, square columns, and a diamond-patterned railing. The main entrance is at the easternmost bay. The nine-light glazed wood door has flanking, three-light sidelights and a large transom. Windows are both one-over-one and two-over- two double hung wood sash.

The interior of the Letcher House has been rehabilitated into modern office space, though the building retains its original central hall plan. Fireplace surrounds have Victorian detailing, including large brackets that mimic the exterior roof cornice modillions. Original stairs, five-panel doors, and four- panel chamfered doors have also been retained. Floors are covered with wall- to-wall carpeting throughout the building.

Both the exterior and interior of 305 Letcher Avenue have good integrity. The overall mass, form, fenestration patterns, and floor plan have been retained. Major character-defining features, such as the windows, doors, fireplace surrounds, and wood trim, have been preserved within the modern office spaces.

Samuel Houston Letcher

Samuel Houston Letcher was a very significant person from an outstanding family. He was son of the Civil War-era Virginia governor, John Letcher, a great-grandson of Sam Houston, and brother of Greenlee Davidson Letcher. Sam Letcher was a VMI cadet at the start of the Civil War, and fought in Company D of the VMI Battalion at the Battle of New Market on 15 May 1864. After VMI was destroyed by General Hunter in 1864, Sam Letcher joined other cadets who went to Richmond to fight the Union Army in the Virginia Militia, and returned to Lexington after the war, where he graduated from VMI in 1869 as valedictorian. Later, he became a circuit judge, a State senator, a member of the VMI Board of Visitors from 1881 to 1882, and was president of the VMI Board of Visitors from 1889 to 1898.

Sam's brother Greenlee Letcher was also a VMI graduate in the Class of 1886. He was chairman of the VMI Alumni Association in 1897 and raised funds for the statue "Virginia Mourning Her Dead" when Maggie Freeland (of the Freeland House) requested funds for the statue.

II.C.8. VMI Foundation (Neikirk Hall/Blair House) - 304 Letcher Avenue

In 1872, VMI faculty member Colonel William Blair built a house next to the Archer House, another early house in the neighborhood. It was on the trail between VMI and Washington & Lee, which is now 304 Letcher Avenue, just inside the present VMI Post Gates. Known today as Neikirk Hall, the property was purchased by VMI in 1920, and used for faculty residences  housing several apartments. Since 1999, the extensively remodeled building has housed the VMI Foundation offices and was re-named Neikirk Hall for Joseph Neikirk, who provided so much assistance to VMI. The original house appears to have been a Gothic cottage with a high front gable facing Letcher Avenue, a Tudor-arched doorway, and elongated semicircular arched windows. The residence known as the Blair House and now Neikirk Hall, is listed as a contributing historical building to the VMI Historic District.

Neikirk Hall is a three-and-a-half story brick Gothic Revival building with a local limestone foundation. The original 1872 three-and-a-half-story portion measures five-bays wide and three-bays deep. When the roof was raised in 1914, the second-story porch was added and the house took on an entirely different appearance with a cross-gabled roof and a Tudor-arched main entrance.

Along the north (rear) façade, a large nine-bay wide and three-bay deep, two-and-a-half-story addition was added to the original residence with a two-story connecting corridor. The rear addition is distinct from the original residence architectural theme, but it does not impact the main façade. The original wood windows remain on the south façade, but have been replaced elsewhere. The historical windows are casement French doors with half-round transoms at the first floor. The replacement windows are four-over-four window panes in a wooden double-hung sash.

The three-story porch is supported on brick piers, and has scrollwork brackets that do not match the other Gothic Revival details, such as the Tudor-arched main entrance. The standing seam metal roof is cross-gabled with prominent north and south dormers. The central entrance has a four-panel wood door with side lights and a transom. There are two internal brick chimneys at both the east and west sides.

The building has good integrity on both the exterior and interior. The windows on all three elevations have been replaced and the porch appears to have been altered. However, the overall form and fenestration patterns have been retained. The Gothic Revival detailing is carried through to the interior with Tudor arches in the entrance foyer and at the parlor fireplace surround. The interior has a center hall plan, and the floor plan and major character-defining features remain. Finishes include window and door trim and four- and five-panel wood doors.

William Barrett Blair

The first builder of the house, William Barrett Blair, was born in Richmond, Virginia, on 25 September 1818, and died in Lexington, Virginia, on 23 March 1883. He was buried in Lexington's Presbyterian Church Cemetery, which became the Stonewall Jackson Memorial Cemetery in 1920. Blair was in the West Point class of 1838, graduating eleventh in his class. He first served as a Second Lieutenant at West Point for two years as a Mathematics Instructor before moving on with the Second Artillery where he became First Lieutenant. In the war with Mexico, Brevet Captain Blair was recognized for gallantry and meritorious conduct at the Battle of Cerro Gordo, Mexico on 18 April 1847.

On 27 September 1850, William B. Blair was made the Captain in the Commissary of Subsistence in the new state of Texas. Stationed in San Antonio, Texas, he was responsible for supplying the provisions for all the US Army installations in Texas. On 18 February 1861, all troops of the United States were ordered to leave the State of Texas and Captain Blair returned to Washington, D.C.

William Blair's commission was rescinded on 14 May 1861 and he was nominated by Governor Letcher of Virginia to the rank of Colonel in the Commissary General of Subsistence for the State of Virginia. In August 1861, he resigned to become a major in the Confederate Army and was attached to the Department of the Trans-Mississippi. He later served in 1863 in the Adjutant General, Headquarters, in Arkansas.

After the Civil War, Colonel Blair was unanimously called by the VMI Board of Visitors to the Chair of Natural and Experiment Philosophy, the position held by General "Stonewall" Jackson before the Civil War. Blair taught at VMI until he retired in 1876.

Joseph Dillard Neikirk

Named for Neikirk Hall, Joseph Dillard Neikirk was born in Lynchburg, Virginia, on 6 August 1911, attended the Augusta Military Academy (AMA) about 80 miles north of Lynchburg, Virginia, graduating second in his class in 1928 and was involved in many activities while at AMA. Neikirk later graduated with a Bachelor of Arts degree from VMI in 1932, where he was a company commander and editor-in-chief of the "The Bomb" yearbook. Following a year's service at the Institute as a sub-professor in Spanish and Tactical Officer, he entered the sales field of the fashion accessory business. He served as a sales manager for several principal firms in this business and later formed his own national sales agency with headquarters in New York City. During World War II, Neikirk volunteered and served four-and-a-half years in the U.S. Army and attained the rank of major in the adjutant general's corps. He began his military service in 1942 as a second lieutenant in the field artillery.

In 1955, Neikirk retired as a senior sales executive to become the VMI Foundation's first full-time Executive Vice President and continued in that position until 1978. The 1975-76 VMI Foundation report states, "Under the imaginative and able direction of Mr. Neikirk, the VMI Foundation enjoyed great growth and expansion from 1955 to 1966. Sound business methods, public relations, organization and communications contributed to the doubling of contributions of the previous decade." Neikirk proclaimed that the strength of the VMI Foundation is built upon a tripod that lies on alumni, parents and friends of VMI, and whose support allows the Foundation to coordinate the multitude of scholarships, awards, funds, and other programs.

Among other accomplishments, Neikirk established "Parents Weekend" and the "Parents Council" as beneficial events for cadets. He felt that giving parents the ability to see how and where cadets live, and meet the faculty and administration, helps parents understand their children better, especially the changes in their lifestyles under the VMI system.

Between 1961 and 1964, Neikirk took on the added position of Executive Vice President of the Marshall Foundation, and was in charge of raising the $600,000 necessary for construction of the Marshall museum and library building. He considered this construction a tribute to perhaps VMI's most distinguished graduate, General George C. Marshall.

Neikirk had given almost half of his life to VMI when he died at age 78 in Lynchburg, Virginia on 20 April 1990, and was buried there in the Old City Cemetery. A memorial service was held for Neikirk on 6 May 1990 in VMI's Jackson Memorial Hall. Even after moving to Lynchburg after his retirement, the Neikirks maintained a rented apartment in Lexington and visited often until illness overtook him. It is stated that their love for VMI and for Lexington kept them coming back.

II.C.9. VMI Protocol Office - 303 Letcher Avenue

The duplex dwelling at 303 Letcher Avenue is located between the VMI Police Department and the VMI Human Resources houses. John D. Letcher had owned a lot of the property on South Institute Hill. After his death in 1884, the property was passed to his heirs and the two-and-one-half story vernacular wood-frame duplex residence was built about 1900. It was owned by his heirs, including his daughter Virginia Stevens, who lived there with her husband who was a W&L faculty professor. It was purchased by the VMI Alumni Association in 1945, and then sold to VMI in 1981.

The house was used as a faculty residence until it served as the Human Resources Office from 1986 to 1995. Then, it was vacant for several years until it became the Protocol Office in 1999. The building presently houses the VMI Protocol offices on the lower level and apartments on the higher level. The duplex dwelling at 303 Letcher Avenue is a contributing historic building to the VMI Historic District.

The wood-framed dwelling is supported on a local limestone foundation and clad in horizontal wood siding. The building is square standing two-and-a-half stories on the north front façade and three-and-a-half stories on the south face, with 8 bedrooms and 4.5 bathrooms. The hipped roof is covered in standing seam metal roofing. The roof drains to a perimeter gutter with downspouts at all four corners. Front-gabled dormers are located on the roof at the north and south. Internal brick chimneys rise through the east and west section of the roof. An exterior brick chimney stands at the east façade.

The north main façade has a one-story, shed-roofed porch that extends across the face of the building. The porch is supported by Neoclassical styled round columns. Two main entrances are located at the center of the north façade. Each entrance has a three-panel wood door with three-light glazing. Windows are modern double-hung replacement sash fitted with exterior storm windows. The windows are set singly or in pairs. The rear south façade has three stories of wood porches and balconies.

The interior of 303 Letcher Avenue has been preserved while adapting the rooms for office space. Each duplex section has a side hall in the center and rooms leading off to the east and west. Character-defining features have been retained, including classically styled fireplace surrounds and wood trim at doors and windows with bull's eye molding. Some original doors remain, including pocket doors, with original door hardware.

II.B.10. VMI Residence (Letcher House) (Absent) – 302 Letcher Avenue

The house at 302 Letcher Avenue west of Neikirk Hall was built in 1907 and demolished in 1998. The house was built by Greenlee Letcher and later owned by his brother Brooke D. Letcher, both sons of John Letcher. Brooke purchased the house when Greenlee moved across the street to the house at 305 Letcher Avenue which had been owned by his brother Samuel Letcher who died in 1914.

The house at 302 Letcher Avenue was purchased by the VMI Alumni Association in 1945 and converted into an apartment house for VMI faculty. It was acquired by VMI in 1956, and still used for VMI faculty. By 1995, there were multiple issues within and outside the house, so it was unoccupied after that time. With lots of reviews of the house, it was estimated that restoration would cost more than $500,000, so the house was demolished in 1998.

Greenlee Letcher

Greenlee Letcher was born on 19 July 1867 in Lexington, Virginia, the son of former Virginia Governor John Letcher. Greenlee graduated at VMI in the class of 1886, and became a lawyer like his father. He provided significant support to VMI as president of the VMI Alumni Association Board from 1894 to 1901. He gave primary support for the statue "Virginia Mourning Her Dead" honoring the ten cadets died from the 1864 Battle of New Market and the statue of the first VMI superintendent Francis H Smith.

Miss Margaret W. Freeland was president of the New Market Memorial Association formed at the home of Greenlee Letcher on 28 May 1897, and requested funding support from Greenlee for the "Virginia Mourning Her Dead" statue. As president of the VMI Alumni Association, he gained support and sent a letter to sculptor Sir Moses Ezekiel in Italy, which resulted in the statue in 1903.

While no plan was developed for the statue of Francis Smith, Greenlee became involved in 1916. Sending a letter to Ezekiel for this statue, Ezekiel responded almost immediately to Greenlee, agreeing to make the sculpture. Unfortunately, before Ezekiel had an opportunity to work on the statue, he died in 1917, and a new sculptor Ferruccio Legnaioli was selected in 1930. Greenlee died on 12 August 1954 and was buried in the Stonewall Jackson Memorial Cemetery in Lexington, Virginia.

II.C.11. VMI Police Office (Bachelor Officers' Quarters) - 301 Letcher Avenue

The VMI Police Office Department at the corner of 301 Letcher Avenue and Maiden Lane is the most westward VMI building, just inside the Limits Gate included in the picture. The Classical Revival style brick building with a two-story portico reflects the prevailing classical architectural taste at Washington & Lee University next to VMI.

The initial building was constructed in c. 1875 as a private home for Mr. Hay, and was sold in 1925 to Washington and Lee University for a Kappa Alpha fraternity house. The main north façade has a full two-story portico supported by four Tuscan columns that were added in 1925 when it became the Kappa Alpha fraternity house. It was later purchased by VMI in 1960 and named Bachelor Officers' Quarters, as it was used as a residence for VMI faculty members. The building is now used for faculty housing and offices for the VMI Police Department. The building is listed as a contributing historic building for the VMI Historic District.

The building is a painted brick structure on a local limestone foundation. Built into the slope of the South Institute Hill, the building is two stories tall at the north façade and four stories tall on the south. The overall form is a rectangular block with flanking wings on the southeast and southwest, and a two-story shed-roofed porch on the west façade. The main entrance for the VMI Police Office Department is located on the western side under the porch.

The main roof is hipped and covered with standing seam metal roofing. Internal chimneys rise from the center and south end of the roof. Windows are typically six-over-six or four-over-four window panes in double-hung wooden sashes. The north façade windows have louvered shutters.

The interior first floor retains the original layout, and historic finishes such as the fireplace surrounds, stairs, doors, and window and door trims. The floors have been covered with wall-to-wall carpeting. In the basement and upper floor areas, original radiators, baseboard and chair rail trim, door and window trim, and some five-panel doors have been retained, and wood windows and doors have also been preserved. The basement floor plan has been modified to accommodate its current use for the VMI Police Office Department.

II.C.12. VMI Construction Office (Freeland House) - 320 Institute Hill

The house at 320 Institute Hill, originally known as the Freeland House, is now the VMI Construction Office. It sits on the slope below Maury-Brooke Hall, and across Main Street from the new Corps Physical Training Facility. Constructed in 1899 as a private residence for Miss Margaret W. Freeland, the house was designed by VMI engineering professor Robert A. Marr. She was known as "Miss Maggie" to VMI cadets. She first connected with the VMI cadets in 1875 and became known as the "VMI Matron". The house was acquired by VMI in 1911 after "Miss Maggie" died in 1908. After its purchase by VMI, it was used as a faculty residence until it became used for the Construction Office.

The three-and-one-half story wood-frame residence is a Queen Anne style house. It was built on a masonry foundation of local limestone and brick, and is clad in horizontal wood siding. The exterior wood cladding, doors, windows, slate roofing, and decorative ornaments extending from the roof have been retained. The overall floor plan and historical finishes have also been retained.

The building has a prominent circular tower atop the center of the east façade. Measuring five-bays wide and three-bays deep, the house stands three-and-a-half stories tall. The slate roof has sloping sides over the house, and the gables under the principal ends of the roofs project to the north and west. The gables have ornamental wood shingle and crossing wood braces to support the roof. An iron ornament decorates the top of the cone-shaped roof over the eastern tower. The semi-circular entrance porch is off-centered, and the gable under the porch roof points to the east.

The windows are two-over-two window panes in double-hung wood sashes. Exterior storm windows were added with louvered shutters fixed to the exterior walls. The double doors at the central main entrance have large plate glass glazing. The main entrance is accessed by concrete steps with modern handrails.

The interior of the house has a large central stair hall with rooms to the north and south. Elaborate newel posts and arched partitions are typical in the three-story main stairwell. Rooms are finished with wood floors and heavy Victorian era wood trim. Original four-panel doors, sliding doors, and ornate door hardware remain. Internal brick chimneys are located in the center and south ends of the house, set in corners with beveled mantelpiece mirrors, tiled insets, and decorative columns. Both the exterior and interior of Freeland House have good integrity, and the building is a contributing resource for the VMI Historic District.

Margaret W. Freeland ("Miss Maggie")

Margaret Freeland, for whom the house was named, first made contact with VMI in 1875 when she was 19. The Corps of Cadets was in Richmond to take part in the unveiling ceremonies of the statue of Stonewall Jackson on Monument Avenue. While attending church in Richmond, two cadets were attracted to two girls in the congregation who were Maggie and Nannie Freeland. They met, and the cadets obtained a promise from the two ladies to attend the next VMI commencement. True to their promise, they came to commencement in 1876, chaperoned by their mother. At Christmas, Maggie sent a box to VMI. Among many delicious things that the box contained was a large jar of brandy peaches. The First Class (seniors) was on pledge not to drink anything alcoholic, so a conversation was taken with Superintendent Smith, and he gave permission to eat the peaches.

Maggie came back to the 1877 commencement and, from that time forward, she became one of the best friends that the cadets ever had. Even before building the Freeman House, it is clear she cared about VMI cadets as the picture taken in 1891 shows a group of cadets with "Miss Maggie" and Miss Poor.

In addition to her caring for the current cadets, she created the New Market Memorial Association in 1897 to honor the cadets killed at New Market. Her efforts led to the statue "Virginia Mourning Her Dead" located in front of Jackson Arch in 1903. It was moved to Letcher Avenue in front of Nichols Hall when the Stonewall Jackson statue replaced it in 1912. More information is provided about her pursuit of the statue "Virginia Mourning Her Dead" in the article IV.A.2. She died in Lexington on 13 May 1908 at the age of 51, and was buried at the Hollywood Cemetery in her hometown of Richmond, Virginia. She was buried on 15 May to honor the cadets who were lost at the Battle of New Market on 15 May 1864.

II.C.13   Diamond Hill – Brooke and Smith Houses – 501 and 503 Brooke Lane

Diamond Hill is a slope of land south of Main Street beyond Foster Stadium. The area was previously known as "Freedmen's Hill" because of the large number of freed African-Americans who settled at the bottom of the slope along Main Street after the Civil War. Two twin wood-framed cottages were built on Diamond Hill in the late 1800's by John Brooke and Francis Smith using the Gothic Revival style popularized by A. J. Davis and the book for house patterns written by A.J. Downing. These were the first faculty residences outside the VMI Post, but both are now owned by VMI.

The Gothic Revival cottages are wood-framed structures clad in vertical wood siding, with a local limestone foundation. The houses are two stories tall, three-bays wide, and two-bays deep, with additions behind. The houses have slanted roofs with metal panels that come together at a ridge, creating triangular walls under the ends of the roof called a gable.

Internal chimneys are located at the east and west ends of the main house. A one-story, roofed porch extends across most of the north façade. Windows consist of six-over-six and four-over-four window panes in double-hung wood sashes. A prominent triple window is located in the center gable on the north façade and the historical main entrance below the porch roof includes double-glazed wood doors.

The interiors have a center hall plan with two rooms on both the east and west sides. Significant original features remain including fireplace surrounds, wood floors, staircases, wood trim, and doors. The original wood surrounding the fireplaces have been stripped to bare wood and finished with a transparent varnish with excellent conditions. Doors date to various periods of construction and appear to be original. The kitchen and bathrooms have been updated with new systems and finishes.

The first residence was built in 1875 by Colonel John Mercer Brooke, whose location was named 501 Brooke Lane. Brooke taught physics at VMI from 1866-1899 and resided in this house until his death in 1906. The Brooke House is located on a small lane that runs south from North Main Street, past Kilbourne Hall, and then climbs the Diamond Hill slope. The house overlooks VMI athletic

areas in the South Post, and the house was purchased by VMI in 1950. The Brooke House is considered an historic building within the VMI Historic District.

In 1885, Superintendent Francis Smith built a twin cottage at 503 Brooke Lane intended for his retirement. It was clearly influenced by the earlier Brooke cottage constructed in 1875. However, Smith did not move into the house until he retired on 1 January 1890 and he died just three months later. The Smith

house was deeded to VMI in 1902, twelve years after Smith's death, and has served for faculty housing since that time. The Smith House has good integrity with the interior floor plan and historical character-defining features, such as original trim, fireplaces, stairs, doors, and windows, which have been retained.

The twin Brooke and Smith cottages have minor differences, and the largest are the additions behind the principal houses. At the southwest corner of the Brooke House is a two-story, one-bay deep addition. This addition is appropriately sized and was sited to the rear of the house. It does not alter the overall shape and form of the initial building, and the main entrance of the addition is through a side door on the west façade. Similar to the Brooke House, the Smith House also has a two-story, one-bay deep projection and a one-story addition at the southeast corner. The front porches are the same, but the stairs up to the porch in the Brooke House are in the north middle of the porch while the front porch on the Smith House has the stairs on the east side.

III. VMI Athletic Facilities

This section addresses the named athletic facilities north and south of the VMI Post used for baseball, lacrosse, soccer, football, basketball and track.

III.A.   North Post Athletic Facilities

Athletic facilities were not built on the north Post of VMI until the 1960's, except for a few tennis courts near Woods Creek in 1956. Starting east on Anderson Drive into Woods Creek Valley on the northern side of the VMI Post, there are three named athletic facilities that are closely related -- Patchin Field, Gray-Minor Stadium, and Paulette Hall – for baseball, soccer and lacrosse.

Baseball was the first intercollegiate sport played at VMI, and started in 1866. The baseball games were initially played on the Parade Ground until 1922 when the games moved to a field south of Main Street, pictured to the right. In 1963, two baseball diamonds were built on the northern VMI Post atop the Woods Creek stream, which passed underneath the baseball fields through a large culvert.   Another named athletic facility on the northeastern side of the VMI Post is Jordan's Point, which is all the way to Maury River and is only used for intramural athletics.

III.A.1.   Patchin Field and Patchin Fieldhouse

Patchin Field is located in Woods Creek Valley north of Anderson Drive, and was built in 1963. In 1964, the first baseball games were played in the new ballpark. Patchin Field had two diamonds, and was named in honor of Herb Patchin. The diamond on the western side of Patchin Field served VMI intercollegiate baseball in the 60's, 70's and early 80's, and the other diamond on the east side was used for practice. In the late 80's,

the baseball diamond that had been used for practice became the new playing field after receiving many upgrades, including a complete renovation of the playing surface on both the infield and outfield. This diamond is now Gray-Minor Stadium.

Along with upgrading the east field in the 80's, a Patchin Fieldhouse was built adjacent to the upgraded baseball diamond to provide locker rooms, coach dressing areas, offices, showers, visiting lockers, and an auxiliary training room featuring a taped bench, two whirlpools, and four treatment beds. The upgraded diamond and new fieldhouse were dedicated on 5 April 1988, with Hall of Famer Joe DiMaggio present. Five years later in 2003, additional upgrades began leading to the Gray-Minor Stadium. Soccer and lacrosse games are now played on Patchin Field, which lies west of Gray-Minor Stadium.

Herbert Patchin

"Herb" Patchin was born on 1 August 1902 in Ford City, Pennsylvania. He arrived at VMI as a University of Illinois educated athletic team trainer in 1929 and served at VMI for 34 years. He initially worked at VMI as an athletic team trainer, but was also a major supporter of intramural sports, including water polo in 1932, and making the requirement that all new cadets would learn to swim. He personally looked at physical education at other colleges, including West Point, and felt VMI was second to none.

Patchin was head of the VMI Physical Education Department from 1942 until his death, 21 years later on 4 September 1963. In that position, he converted the physical training course from the Army TC 87 program, designed for heavy combat conditioning, to normal training. He also supported cadets, who were not on intercollegiate teams, but who participated in intramural sports. The Richmond "News Leader" stated in 1946 that the physical education at VMI was "Patchin Works". He was complimented on his many services to VMI, which included use of his own money to help cadets, recruiting outstanding young men for varsity sports, and counseling those cadets who he thought needed advice.

Patchin was also instrumental in supporting VMI's athletic facilities. Some have stated that the first Alumni Stadium for football stood as a proud tribute to Patchin, who worked selflessly to make it built, and he was the inspiration for what became Patchin Field. After 20 years of service, in 1949, Patchin was given an award by the VMI Sportsman Club (now the Keydet Club) in Jackson Memorial Hall with all cadets attending, and the presentation by General Lemuel Shepherd, Class of 1917, for Patchin's outstanding service.

Patchin was later acknowledged as the long-time "dean" of Southern Conference trainers, and one of the 26 original selections to the Helms Hall of Fame for Athletic Trainers. His name is inscribed in the International Sports Shrine, Helms Hall, in Los Angeles, California. After Patchin died, the Alumni Association immediately created the "Herbert Patchin Memorial Scholarship" and, in the spring of 1964, the new baseball diamonds built north of the VMI Post were named for Patchin at the primary suggestion of John Henry Binford "Binnie" Peay, VMI Class of 1929, the father of the present VMI superintendent.

III.A.2. Gray-Minor Stadium and Paulette Hall

Gray-Minor Stadium was constructed on the north side of the VMI Post along Anderson Road, on the former eastern Patchin Field diamond. The ground-breaking construction of the Gray-Minor Stadium began on 9 September 2005 and was completed in 2007. Renovation of the Patchin Field Locker Room Complex, which was named Paulette Hall, began in 2003, and was also completed in 2007.

The Gray-Minor Stadium became the new home for VMI baseball, and it was dedicated along with Paulette Hall on 27 March 2007 at the opening of the 2007 season. The new baseball

stadium was named for Elmon Gray and Gil Minor, VMI graduates in 1948 and 1963, and the revised locker room was named Paulette Hall for Bill Paulette, VMI Class of 1969. The two new facilities were dedicated with the three VMI alumni pictured to the right -- Gil Minor, Bill Paulette, and Elmon Gray – who worked together and made significant contributions to renovate these baseball facilities. The three alumni echoed their former VMI baseball experience when Paulette tossed the first ball, with Minor acting as catcher and Gray at bat.

As a part of the Gray-Minor Stadium construction, the former Patchin Field received another upgrade, with new fencing raising to 15 feet around the entire outfield. The stadium provided seating for 1400 fans, including 700 chair-back seats, plus covered batting cages, a state-of-the-art scoreboard with a videoboard and a first-class press box. In addition to features like rebuilt dugouts, and professional scout and handicapped seating behind home plate, the stadium provided a concession stand and large restrooms. Gray-Minor Stadium also included stadium light towers which gave VMI an opportunity to host the program's first baseball night games.

.

Elmon Taylor Gray

Elmon Gray was born in Hague, Virginia on 1 May 1925, and died in Richmond, Virginia on 27 September 2011 at age 86. He entered VMI in 1942, in the Class of 1946, but left VMI in 1944 to join the US Navy where he served on a minesweeper in the South Pacific. He left the Navy in 1946, and attended the University of Richmond for two semesters under the Naval V-12 program. He re-entered VMI and graduated in June 1948. Gray was a strong member of the varsity baseball team.

After graduation, Gray joined his father's Gray Lumber Company in Waverly, Virginia. He became the president in 1953 and expanded its operations to real estate development in the Richmond suburbs. In 1992, in an effort to diversify its investments, the family elected to exchange a large portion of its timberland for commercial real estate and form an in-house management team. The company changed its name to Gray Land and Timber Company. While leading the company as chairman of the board, the company changed its name to GrayCo, Inc.

While president of his company, he was elected to the Virginia Senate in 1971, and held the seat for 20 years which his father had held for the prior 30 years. Gray was chairman of the Senate Education and Health Committee, and served on the transportation, commerce and labor committees. He was also on the Senate Finance Committee where it is reported he was a significant supporter for VMI's tax funding. Virginia Governor Bob McDonnell said Mr. Gray's devotion to VMI showed that he "was a strong supporter of Virginia's world-class institutions of higher education."

Gray also served on numerous boards including the Bank of Waverly, James River Bankshares, First & Merchants National Bank, Virginia Electric Power Company, the Universal Leaf Tobacco Company, the Sussex County School, and Elon University. He had a passion for charitable fund-raising and helped raise money for various organizations including VMI, Elon University, Boy Scouts of America, Appomattox Regional Governor's School, Virginia Historical Society, National D-Day Memorial at Bedford, Stuart Hall, and the Southeast 4-H Educational Center.

He was a devoted alumnus, helping to raise millions of dollars for VMI, and serving as president of the Board of Visitors from 1964 to 1966, and president of the VMI Alumni Association from 1971 to 1973. In 2009, Gray received VMI's prestigious Harry F. Byrd Jr. Public Service Award for a life of distinguished public service and for best-representing VMI's core values of "selflessness, integrity, patriotism, and courage."

George Gilmer Minor III

Gil Minor was born in Richmond, Virginia on 12 October 1940. He attended VMI and graduated in the Class of 1963, with a Bachelor of Art degree in history. He was co-captain of the varsity football team that won the 1962 Southern Conference Championship, and received Southern Conference Honorable Mention. He was also co-captain of the varsity baseball team and named 1st Team catcher in the All-Southern Conference.

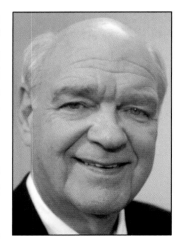

After graduation in 1963, he joined Hanover County-based Owens & Minor, Inc., a family-owned medical products distributor that expanded from a regional, Sun Belt distributor to a national company that not only supplied essential medical tools to hospitals but also provided logistics services to the health care industry. Gil Minor was the fourth generation of his family to work for Owens & Minor founded in 1882, and was named for the company's co-founder, his great grandfather. He earned a Master of Business Administration (MBA) from the Colgate-Darden School at the University of Virginia in 1966.

At Owens & Minor, he worked in sales, operations and management capacities before becoming president in 1981 and CEO from 1984 to 2005. He retired as board chairman in 2013, when he became chairman emeritus. He still keeps office hours at Owens & Minor's headquarters in Mechanicsville, Virginia. In 1999, he relinquished the president's title, remaining chairman of the Board and CEO until he became the non-executive chairman of the Board in 2005.

Minor has also been active in many civic, charitable, financial and industry organizations. He was a member of the boards for Virginia Commonwealth University's (VCU) Massey Cancer Center, VCU's School of Business Foundation, the University of Virginia's School of Nursing, the Virginia Biotechnology Research Park, the Virginia Health Care Foundation, Crestar Financial Corporation, Richford Holdings, and SunTrust Banks.

He was also a member of the Virginia Business Higher Education Council and Virginia Business Council. His leadership has earned him wide recognition, including being named Virginia Industrialist of the Year in 2001 and receiving the B'nai B'rith National Healthcare Award in 2004.

Minor's service to VMI has been wide-ranging. He was on the VMI Keydet Club Board from 1984 to 1987, a member of the VMI Foundation's Board of Trustees 1993 to 2000 and president from 1997 to 2000, and on the VMI Board of Visitors from 2000 to 2008 and president from 2005 to 2008.

Paulette Hall

Paulette Hall was constructed on the north side of the VMI Post along Anderson Road, adjacent to the Gray-Minor baseball stadium, and built by Bill Paulette's general contracting company, KBS. Construction of Paulette Hall began in 2003, a renovation of

the Patchin Field Locker Room Complex. Paulette Hall was dedicated along with Gray-Minor Stadium on 27 March 2007, and named for Bill Paulette due to his significant contribution to the new building and VMI. Reconstruction included not only locker rooms for baseball, but also facilities for men and women's soccer teams, men's lacrosse teams, a locker room for visitors, a training and storage room, and a room for umpires and officials. The locker rooms were also fitted with audio and visual equipment.

William Aubrey Paulette

Bill Paulette was born in South Hill, Virginia, on 26 September 1947. He attended VMI and graduated in the Class of 1969. Paulette earned a Bachelor of Science degree in civil engineering and he lettered in both varsity football and varsity baseball. After his graduation, he served in the U.S. Army from 1969 to 1972. Subsequently, he was the area sales manager for Republic Steel in Richmond, Virginia.

In 1975, he founded the construction company KBS in Richmond, and has been its president from 1975 to 2017. With more than 4 decades of construction experience, KBS has built numerous multi-million dollar projects in Central Virginia. Paulette was also a co-founder and board member of the Bank of Richmond, now Hampton Roads Bankshares Inc., where he remains a director. In his civic efforts, he was a former board member of the Virginia Board for Contractors; a former chairman of the Henrico County Community Services Board; and a former member of the Make-A-Wish Foundation Board.

In support of VMI, Bill has made significant contributions, served on the VMI Board of Visitors from 2002 to 2010, served on the VMI Keydet Club's Board of Governors from 1997 to 2002, and was its president from 2011 to 2016.

III.A.3. Jordan's Point Field

Jordan's Point Field is located at the most northeast section of the VMI Post, sitting aside the Maury River. The athletic field was created in 2004, and named for John Jordan. Because the field is so recent, there is not much VMI athletic history about it; however, there is significant history about the location. While Lexington owns the land, VMI contracted to build the multi-purpose field. VMI has exclusive use of the field on weekday afternoons during the academic year for intramural and club sports.

The field will be available for other uses by Lexington on weekends and during the summer months. No permanent structures, goals or goal posts will be installed, and all improvements were done to ensure they would not distract from the natural setting of Jordan's Point. VMI and Lexington have established a win-win memorandum regarding use of the field. The city provided the property, including water, electrical services, and an irrigation system. VMI paid for construction of the field. The city also maintains portable toilets on the site and mowing.

Jordan's Point had long been an important location for transportation in Rockbridge County, with a ford providing river crossing at this location as early as the 1740s. The John Jordan family constructed a toll bridge in 1834 and controlled the river crossing. Jordan also established on Jordan's Point a foundry and forge, as well as flour mills. Jordan was a nineteenth century pioneer in construction, iron industry, and transportation systems in western Virginia. The hub of Lexington's nineteenth-century commercial and industrial development was located at the confluence of the North River (now Maury River) and Woods Creek.

A biography of John Jordan is included in the II.A.1. "Jordan's Point"/"Stono"/Turman House article.

III.B. South Post Athletic Facilities

South of Main Street, at the bottom of Diamond Hill, the athletic facilities include Cormack Hall (west of Kilbourne Hall), the Foster Stadium and Alumni Memorial Field, Clarkson-McKenna Hall (attached to and behind Foster Stadium), Fiorini Field behind Clarkson-McKenna Hall, Cameron Hall (east of Foster Stadium), and a new large athletic training facility, including an indoor track and swimming pool, named the Corps Physical Training Facility.

III.B.1. Cormack Hall

Cormack Hall is located south of Main Street, west of Kilbourne Hall. This building was named for Coach Walter Cormack and, not only used for indoor track and basketball, but was first an indoor horse arena when the building was constructed in 1941.   In 1948, the Army mechanized its cavalry and deleted horses, and VMI released its horses. The building then became home for VMI track and basketball, and was nicknamed "The Pit".

After basketball games moved to Cameron Hall in 1981, Cormack Hall continued to host indoor track events. It had a 200-meter banked APS TARTAN track and locker rooms for both the VMI

men's and women's track teams. In 1986, the building was named for Walter B. Cormack for his long time as a very successful track coach. Renovations of Cormack Hall began in 2014, to remove the indoor track and provide new wrestling courts, other mat sports, and seating for 750 spectators. A new building west of Cameron Hall named the Corps Physical Training Facility was completed in 2016 and now provides the indoor track.

Cormack Hall is home to VMI's Department of Physical Education, and provides numerous Physical Education classes. It also has an art exercise laboratory helping studies and research for VMI's newly founded Exercise Science Minor, which is designed to provide cadets with a comprehensive introduction to the basis of exercise and fitness. It will prepare cadets to be eligible to sit for the American College of Sports Medicine Health and Fitness Instructor Certification Examination or the National Strength and Conditioning Association Certified Strength and Conditioning Specialist, and Tactical Strength and Conditioning Facilitator Examinations.

Walter Bernard Cormack

Walt Cormack was born in Mecklenburg County, North Carolina, on 8 September 1918. He graduated with a Bachelor's Degree in Geology from the University of South Carolina (USC) in 1939, and he was captain of the long distance track team. After graduation, he served on the USC faculty and worked for the Santee-Cooper power company as an archeologist during its construction, and discovered mastodon and mammoth teeth. In 1942, Walt joined the U.S. Army and served during World War II until 1946. In 1949, after graduate study at Johns-Hopkins University, Walt joined VMI as an assistant professor of geology and became the track coach succeeding Colonel "Son" Read until health forced his retirement on 31 December 1974. Major Cormack died on 30 March 1975, at the age of 57, after a long chronic illness.

Considered the father of indoor track in the South, Cormack and his ability and character earned repeated informal recognition from state and national leaders in the track and field sports. He initiated the VMI Winter Relays in 1951 and developed them into one of the top annual sports events in the Southeast. The Virginia Association of the U.S. Track and Field Federation gave him its first service award in 1968 and, in 1973, the Virginia Intercollegiate Track and Field Coaches Association established an award in his honor.

In conjunction with the VMI Winter Relays on 1 February 1986, ceremonies were held to name the VMI field house in memory of the late Major Walter B. Cormack, and the VMI Keydet Club endowment fund provides the Coach Walter B. Cormack Memorial Track Scholarship. His track and cross country teams won 13 Southern Conference titles and 30 state championships, the most titles any coach in VMI history ever collected.

III.B.2 H.M. "Son" Read '16 Memorial Track

Surrounding Alumni Memorial Field in front of Foster Stadium is an outdoor track named the H.M. "Son" Read '16 Memorial Track, dedicated in 1971. The first track meet at VMI was an intramural type event on the Parade Ground at Finals in 1889, and continued in future Finals. When the VMI inter-collegiate track meets began circa 1916, the outdoor meets were held on a cinder track close to the present track.

In 1986, the "Son" Read track was converted from 6 to 8 lanes, and changed from 440 yards to 400 meters.   The funds for the construction of the track, high jump, steeplechase water jump, and long jump pit were secured completely through donation to the VMI Foundation, Inc.   A committee, partially made up of Colonel Read's former athletes, was responsible for selecting the funds.   Completion of the project along with renovations and subsequent resurfacings gave VMI one of the best tracks in the Southeast.

Hernando Money "Son" Read

"Son" Read was born in Dallas, Texas, on 28 February 1897. He was a member of the VMI Class of 1916, and graduated with a Bachelor of Arts degree in English.   After graduation, he joined the English Department as a professor of English, and his teaching ranged over Shakespeare, business law, literature, and public speaking. Colonel Read also served as director of publicity and editor of the Alumni Review, and advisor to various cadet publications.

He was also a track star and got the training at VMI that led him to be a track team coach.   Starting in 1917, he served as an assistant track coach, became the head coach in 1918, and started a cross-country track team in 1922. The VMI track team won the 1942 Virginia state championship as the climax of an undefeated season, coached by the man who did so much at VMI for years.

"Son" Read coached indoor, outdoor, and cross-country track until his retirement in 1954.   Even after his retirement, he would still be present at track meets serving as an official. Colonel Read was also an assistant athletic director and served in other athletic events officiating games and matches for intercollegiate football, wrestling, boxing, and swimming for many years. He served VMI from his graduation until his death on 15 July 1968, at the age of 71, and was buried in the "Stonewall" Jackson Cemetery.

On 20 November 1971, during halftime of the VMI-University of Chattanooga football game, VMI's new Uniroyal track was dedicated to the late Colonel Read and named "H.M. 'Son' Read '16 Memorial Track".   A bronze memorial plaque for Read was placed at the finish line of the track followed by an acceptance speech by the VMI Superintendent General Richard L. Irby. At that time, the "H.M. 'Son' Read '16 Memorial Track" scholarship was also created and has continued to the present.

III.B.3. Foster Stadium and Alumni Memorial Field

Foster Stadium and Alumni Memorial Field are located immediately south of Main Street, adjacent east of Cameron Hall. The first VMI football game was played in 1889 on the Parade Ground, an unlevel ridged and hard ground that led to numerous injuries, and this led to establishing Alumni Field in 1921. The field was graded level for football and concrete bleachers were built north of the field adjacent to Main Street. The bleachers still lie across from the first

stadium built in 1962. Colonel William Couper, VMI Class of 1904, and Captain Montgomery Corse, VMI Class of 1885, initiated and headed the proposal to VMI alumni to establish a new football field. VMI alumni raised $60,000 to build Alumni Memorial Field, and it was dedicated to VMI cadets who died in World War I. The first football game played on Alumni Memorial Field was against Roanoke College on 24 September 1921, and VMI won 13-0. The field was dedicated on 15 October 1921 when VMI played against the University of Virginia and lost 14-7.

Until 1962, seats for attendees to watch football, baseball and track consisted only of the concrete stands built in 1921, which provided about 2500 seats. A new stadium was completed in 1962 containing 54 rows, towering 173 feet high, and provided a seating capacity of 10,000. Fiberglass seats were installed in 1974 and refurbished in 1985. After becoming head of the VMI Physical Education Department, Herb Patchin was instrumental in the planning of VMI's athletic facilities, and some have stated that Patchin worked selflessly to see Alumni Stadium built.

In an effort to further upgrade the Institute's athletic facilities, Alumni Stadium received a major facelift in 2006 thanks to the generous contributions of P. Wesley Foster, Jr., VMI Class of 1956. These renovations were formally dedicated on 29 September 2006, and the upgraded stadium was named Foster Stadium. The facelift included better seats with a new scoreboard and a jumbotron, a very large video display screen. New game-day locker rooms and a new

concourse were created under the stands with several fan-friendly amenities including new concession stands and new restrooms. The new Foster Stadium featured an entrance plaza (pictured to the left) with a plaque for Foster and his name over the wrought iron gates. The entrance includes permanent ticket booths, restrooms, and concessions.

Paul Wesley Foster, Jr.

Wes Foster was born on 25 November 1933 in Forest Park, Georgia. He graduated in the VMI Class of 1956 with a Bachelor of Arts degree in English. He was a varsity football player and served on the Honor Court. After graduation, Foster, delayed his military duty for one year and worked for Kaiser Aluminum in the Chicago office. He then entered the U.S. Army and served for two years in West Germany.

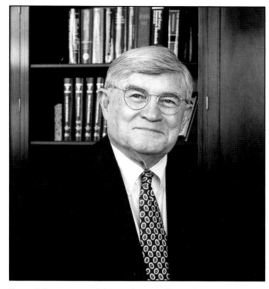

After leaving the Army, Foster traveled around Europe for a year before returning to the United States and took back his job with Kaiser Aluminum. While selling aluminum building products to homebuilders across the United States, he met the owner of Minchew Corporation, a home building company in Northern Virginia, who was also from Georgia. After working there for three years, Foster began his real estate career in 1963 as a sales manager and, in 1966, moved to Nelson Realty as vice president of sales.

Foster met Henry Long (a graduate of Virginia Tech) when they were both working on a project in Northern Virginia and, in 1968, they founded Long & Foster. They flipped a coin to choose the firm's name. Long won and got his name first in the firm's name, while Foster became the president. Long pursued commercial business, and Foster was more interested in residential business. After 11 years, in 1979, Foster bought Long's share of the company after Merrill Lynch wanted to buy the firm. The name of the firm changed to Long & Foster Companies, a family of businesses in the real estate and financial services industries, and included Long & Foster Real Estate, the nation's largest privately owned real estate company and the largest global affiliate of Christie's International Real Estate, Prosperity Mortgage, Mid-States Title, and Long & Foster Insurance. Foster served as both the chief executive officer and board chairman, with the firm headquartered in Chantilly, Virginia, with offices in seven states in the mid-Atlantic region.

Foster was very dedicated to VMI, and received the VMI Foundation's Distinguished Service Award in 2003. He had served on the VMI Foundation board from 1990 to 1996. He was also on the Keydet Club Board of Governors from 1983 to 1989, and the VMI Board of Visitors from 2007 to 2015. He also created scholarships, including several that provide grant-in-aid assistance to football players who "walk on" to the VMI team and who don't have full scholarships, as well as a disciplinary fund for the Department of English and Fine Arts.

III.B.4. Clarkson-McKenna Hall

The VMI football operations building, Clarkson-McKenna Hall, bears the names of Blandy Clarkson and John McKenna, both outstanding football coaches at VMI. This building was completed in 1988, and is connected to the south side of Foster Stadium. Clarkson-McKenna Hall consists of four levels, with the main entrance to the building on the ground level, near the concession area behind the Foster Stadium. A ramp from the back of the building leads down onto a Sprinturf practice field, named Fiorini Field.

The first level includes a lobby area and an elevator to take individuals to the upper three levels. Also on the first level are equipment and laundry rooms, and all mechanical heating and air conditioning equipment of the building. The second level includes the football locker room and training room. Included in the Foster renovation project in 2006 was an expansion of the locker room, and the addition of the weight room and the athletic training facility. Coaches' offices, and meeting and film rooms, are included on the third level. Access to the Superintendent's box is also on this level as well as an enclosed area, the Ferebee Lounge, and an open-air seating arrangement for viewing the football games.

The fourth level consists primarily of the press box, with the center section including newspaper writers and statisticians. Five separate booths flanking this space are used by home and visiting radio crews, VMI and opponents' coaches, the announcer, and the scoreboard, message center, and clock operators. Television crews film from the top of the press box. There is also a lounge and dining area in the rear of the press box, which also serves as a players' lounge during non-game days.

Blandy Benjamin Clarkson

Blandy Benjamin Clarkson was born on 15 March 1890 in Millboro, Virginia, and graduated from VMI in the Class of 1914. He was a Mathematics professor at VMI from 1920 to 1954, and he was the longest serving athletic director in VMI history, having served from 1926 to 1946. Before serving as the VMI Athletic Director, he coached the VMI football team from 1920 through 1926. In his first year as football coach, 1920, the team was undefeated (9 – 0), and was later named the "Flying Squadron". A plaque with all the names of the players on that team hangs in the mezzanine level of Cameron Hall, past the opening doors. He died on 2 December 1954 at the age of 64 and, in 1972, Clarkson was chosen by the Honors Committee to join the VMI Sports Hall of Fame.

John Henry McKenna, Jr.

John McKenna was born on 12 November 1914 in Lawrence, Massachusetts. He lettered three years in football at Villanova University, where he was a standout center for the Wildcats' undefeated squad of 1937. He earned a B.A. in philosophy in 1938. After coaching football at Malvern (Pa.) Prep, Villanova, and Loyola, Los Angeles, McKenna was hired in 1952 at VMI as an assistant coach, and served as the head coach from 1953 to 1965.

McKenna's VMI football teams won four Southern Conference championships and achieved an undefeated season in 1957, as the Keydets went 9-0-1. The team was ranked 20th in the nation. McKenna was a three-time selection as the Southern Conference Coach of the Year. He received a special citation for the VMI Sports Hall of Fame in 1979.

After departing VMI, McKenna served the Georgia Tech Athletic Association from 1966 to 1979. When he first joined the Georgia Tech staff, his initial responsibilities included assistant athletics director, head of physical training, director of intramurals and head freshman football coach. He was promoted to Associate Director of Athletics in 1972.

McKenna died at age 94, on 31 March 2007, in Decatur, Georgia, the same year he was inducted into the Virginia Sports Hall of Fame, and was buried in the Stonewall Jackson Cemetery in Lexington. His most reported quote: "I've never tried to run a popularity contest. I was a tough coach and hopefully a strong and fair administrator. Athletics, like life, requires discipline and sacrifice."

III.B.5. Delany/Fiorini Field

Delaney Field served as VMI's football practice field beginning in the early 1960s behind the football Alumni Field and the bottom of Diamond Hill. The practice field was named for Martin Delaney.

In 1987, Delaney Field was upgraded, including topsoil and seeding, and relocating the tall lights to this field from Patchin Field. In 2006, with the Foster Stadium project, a Sprinturf surface, lights and a scoreboard, were added to Delaney Field to enhance the practice capabilities for several VMI teams and provide a field for lacrosse. The field was renamed Fiorini Field for Al Fiorini on 10 November 2012.

Dr. Martin Donohue Delaney, Jr.

Martin Delaney was born in Alexandria, Virginia, on 5 June 1907. He was a graduate of VMI in the Class of 1928, and earned a Bachelor of Science degree in Chemical Engineering. Later, he earned his medical degree at Georgetown University in 1932, and took over the medical practice that had been started by his father in Alexandria as a surgeon, internist, and pediatrician. He was also a founder of the Circle Terrace Hospital in Alexandria.

In 1947, Delaney began his service to VMI as a volunteer physician with the football team and attended virtually every game, home and away, through 1976. He was an honorary member of the National Athletic Trainers Association, given a special citation by the VMI Sportsman Club Honors Committee in 1972 when the VMI Sports Hall of Fame was inaugurated, and president of the VMI Keydet Club Board from 1969 to 1971. The VMI Keydet Club gave him its Spirit Award when the football practice field was named in his honor. Delaney died on 10 March 1986 at the age of 78.

Albert Edward Fiorini

Al Fiorini was born in Norfolk, Virginia, on 1 February 1942, and graduated from VMI in the Class of 1964 with a Bachelor of Science degree in Civil Engineering. Fiorini was a three-year member of the VMI football team and a Distinguished Military Graduate. After graduation, he served in the U.S. Army for three years, including a tour in Viet-Nam.

After leaving the Army, Fiorini was the founder, president, and chief executive officer of KCC International Inc., a manufacturer of metal roof components and commercial air-conditioning units in Louisville, Kentucky. The football practice field was renamed for Al due to his creation of VMI's largest individually endowed athletic scholarship – "The Albert E. Fiorini '64 Football Scholarship" -- and his other significant donations in support of VMI athletics. He also served on the Keydet Club Board of Governors from 2000 to 2006.

III.B.6. Cameron Hall

Built in 1981, Cameron Hall is located south of Main Street, and west of Alumni Memorial Field. Cameron Hall was named after brothers Bruce Cameron and Dan Cameron, both graduates of VMI, due to their significant contribution to its cost. Cameron Hall seats 5,029 spectators for basketball, and 4,300 for plays, concerts, and VMI's commencement every May. The

first basketball game at Cameron Hall was played on 5 December 1981, and VMI lost to the University of Virginia 76 to 49.

Cameron Hall was not updated until 1995, when it received an extensive facelift that included repainted walls and portals, new railings, and a new floor color scheme. Locker rooms were also renovated, with new carpeting, paint, and a lounge. In 2007, VMI installed a new court donated by Ralph Costen, also a VMI graduate, and was appropriately named "Costen Court". In the summer of 2012, Cameron Hall's Costen Court was refinished and adorned with the signature

Red, Yellow, and White colors of VMI, and the signature VMI spider logo shines brighter than ever at center court.

Cameron Hall also provides VMI athletic department offices, and contains a library, reception area, and five racquetball courts open to cadets in the basement level. Electronic screens were added on the sidelines, as well as a "VMI Keydets" moniker that runs along both baselines under and behind the basket. There are concessions on both ends of the arena.

Sports Hall of Fame

In 1999, a VMI "Wall of Fame" was added to the mezzanine level in Cameron Hall, which features photographs and trophies as a tribute to former VMI members of the VMI Sports Hall of Fame. The VMI Sports Hall of Fame was inaugurated in 1972, when 64 charter members were inducted.

Bruce Barclay Cameron, Jr. and Daniel David Cameron

Bruce Cameron was born in Wilmington, North Carolina, on 6 September 1917, and died on 3 April 2013 at the age of 95. At VMI, Cameron earned a Bachelor of Science degree in Civil Engineering in the Class of 1938, and performed on the pistol and wrestling teams. After graduation, Bruce went to work for MacMillan and Cameron, the family business, which operated a massive service station, garage and auto supply business. In 1941, Bruce joined the U.S. Army. He helped build Camp Davis near Holly Ridge, North Carolina, served as a general's aide at Fort Bliss, Texas, and was later posted to New Guinea. Cameron served in the Army until 1945, and then returned to Wilmington to take his father's position as president of McMillian and Cameron. His father had died in 1944.

Dan Cameron was also born in Wilmington, North Carolina, on 16 October 1921, and died on 2 July 2005, at the age of 83. Dan was also a VMI graduate in the Class of 1942, with a Bachelor of Science degree in Civil Engineering. After graduation, he served in the US Army until 1946. Like his brother Bruce, he was initially assigned to Camp Davis, at Holly Ridge, North Carolina. Later, he took part in the battle at Normandy three days after the invasion on 6 June 1944. He later served in multiple places in Europe, serving as a prison guard at the allied prisoner of war camp in Stuttgart, Germany. After his Army tour, Dan also returned to Wilmington to rejoin his family and work at the McMillian and Cameron Company.

Bruce and Dan worked together, but individually created substantial business achievements and contributed significantly to civic and charitable affairs. For example, in addition to working for the McMillan and Cameron Company, in 1946 Dan was on the transportation committee with the Wilmington Chamber of Commerce, and led the effort to get a four-lane highway on US 17 and a four-lane highway to Charlotte, North Carolina, which is now I-40. A four-lane automobile bridge spanning the Northeast Cape Fear River in New Hanover County, which carries I-40 and US 17, was opened in 2005 and is named the "Dan Cameron Bridge".

In 1954, the Camerons started WECT, Wilmington's first television station. Dan was president of the company until the Camerons sold their interest in 1987. In 1955, Dan was elected mayor of Wilmington, and served for two years until 1957. Also, in 1955, the Cameron brothers purchased island property off the shore of North Carolina and north of Wrightsville Beach to develop Figure Eight Island, which became one of the most expensive and exclusive real estate properties on the Cape Fear coast.

Dan was also instrumental in the formation of the Committee of 100, which helped revitalize industry in the Wilmington area after the departure of the Atlantic Coast Line Railroad, and Bruce sat on several boards of directors, including the Atlantic Pepsi-Cola Bottling Co., the North Carolina National Bank (a corporate predecessor of Bank of America) and Atlantic Telecasting Corporation, which purchased the Wilmington television station WECT from the Camerons.

Bruce and Dan were also significantly involved in civic philanthropy. In addition to funding the construction of Cameron Hall at VMI, Bruce and Dan with other members of their family were major supporters of the University of North Carolina-Wilmington and its primary facility, Cameron Hall, which were named for the Cameron family in 1988. The Cameron family also supported the former St. John's Museum of Art in Wilmington, often through the Bruce B. Cameron Foundation. In 1990, Bruce launched a drive to establish an endowment fund for St. John's Museum. He later donated significant land and funds for a new 40,000-square St. Johns Museum, which opened in 2002, and was renamed the Louise Wells Cameron Art Museum for his wife. Later, in May 2011, the Bruce B. Cameron Foundation offered a $1 million matching grant to the museum.

Bruce Cameron also served as a trustee for the New Hanover Regional Medical Center, and he and his family donated land for the hospital's Urgent Care Center. The Cameron Area Health Education Center was named for Bruce, Dan, and their parents. Bruce was a major donor to Cape Fear Academy, where the Bruce B. Cameron Gym is named in his honor. Bruce also donated land to the Cape Fear Council of Boy Scouts of America, which became the site of the council's headquarters and the Lower Cape Fear Hospice. Over the years, Cameron money went to area churches and to the Brigade Boys and Girls Club.

Cameron Management, Inc. is an investment management company founded in 2000 and based in Wilmington, North Carolina, with a focus on real estate development, brokerage and property management. Cameron Management was established to more effectively manage the investments, businesses and properties of Bruce, Dan and their families.

The Cameron brothers received numerous awards for their philanthropy. In 1998, the Bruce B. Cameron Foundation received a Governor's Business Award; in 2001, "Celebrate Wilmington" presented Bruce and Dan Cameron with lifetime achievement awards; and, in 2003, Bruce and Dan Cameron were the first recipients of the Wilmington Star News Lifetime Achievement Awards. Bruce served on the VMI Foundation from 1976 to 1979 and the VMI's Board of Visitors from 1979 to 1988. Dan served on the VMI Foundation from 1980 to 1988 and the VMI Board of Visitors from 1988 to 1996.

Ralph Lynch Costen, Jr.

Ralph Costen was born in Richmond, Virginia, on 22 May 1948. He was a graduate of VMI in the Class of 1970, with a Bachelor of Art degree in History. He was also on the varsity tennis team. After graduation, he started work with Costen Floors, Inc., a wood-flooring company in Richmond, Virginia, founded by his father in 1948. Later, Ralph became the president and is now the CEO. In 1991, Ralph and his brother-in-law created a sister company, American Floors, which specialized in carpet, vinyl and ceramic. In 2013, Ralph and his son started Creative Flooring Solutions, which concentrates on Property Management and Material Only sales. A year later, Ralph and son joined the national buying group, CCA, and opened Costen Flooring America in Midlothian, which concentrates on retail sales and gives Costen a national buying advantage. Ralph presently served on the VMI Keydet Club Board of Governors beginning in 1985, and was the president from 1999 to 2001.

III.B.7. Corps Physical Training Facility

Although not named for anyone yet, this is a tremendous new facility located south of Main Street and west of Cameron Hall. The building, opened formally in January of 2017, is dual-purpose, as it is used for both track and field, and Corps of Cadets physical training activities. The track is a hydraulic banked, 200-meter oval with two sprint straights and two long/triple jump and vault runways located in the center of the oval. It is believed to be one of only six indoor tracks at the NCAA level with a 200-meter banked hydraulic oval, and one of only two with a Beynon-produced surface.

There are also two high jump areas and two throwing cages located at one end of the venue. The entire facility is wired for video, scoreboard and music. Above the main floor is a flat, 350-meter warm-up track that athletes can use to prepare for their events. The facility also contains full locker rooms, classrooms, coaches and administrative offices, athletic training facilities, and equipment for use by the track and field programs. Also for use by the Corps of Cadets is a rock climbing wall and high climbing ropes. Spectator seating has been estimated at 1,800, plus standing room around the track.

This has also been a fun facility for children and grandchildren of VMI alumni attending the VMI Legacy Day in the spring. They enjoy climbing the rock wall and ropes, running, and more athletic efforts. Four of my grandsons have attended and also enjoyed the science lecture in Mallory Hall and touring VMI.

IV. VMI Arches, Statues, Monuments and Memorials

At the Virginia Military Institute, there are a number of arches, statues, monuments and memorials. There are four arches which provide openings into VMI Barracks which have been named. The first arch was named for George Washington, an opening to the south side of the first barracks built in 1850. The next arch was named for Thomas "Stonewall" Jackson in 1896 when it was built as an opening to the west side of Old Barracks. The next arch was named for George Marshall for an opening to New Barrracks built in 1949. And, the small arch on the west side of Old Barracks leading to Richardson Hall was named for Jonathon Daniels in 2004.

The six statues were created to honor two VMI superintendents, two army generals, one to honor VMI cadets who were lost in the Civil War Battle of New Market in 1864, and the first statue was to honor George Washington. The Washington statue was created and placed in front of Washington Arch in 1856 because of his correlation with the essential VMI "citizen-soldier" feature. The statue "Virginia Mourning Her Dead" was placed on Post in 1903 to honor the 10 VMI cadets who passed away due to fighting in the Battle of New Market. In 1931, a statue was unveiled to honor Francis H. Smith, who was the first superintendent at VMI, and served from 1839 to 1889. The statue is located in front of Smith Hall. A statue named "Spirit of Youth" was unveiled in 1939 in Memorial Garden. It was donated by Mrs. Cocke for the memory of her husband William H. Cocke, who was the fourth VMI superintendent. The two statues named for army generals including Thomas "Stonewall" Jackson, a VMI faculty member and a general in the Confederate Army during the Civil War, and the statue was placed in front of Jackson Arch in 1912. George Marshall, Jr., was a VMI graduate in 1901 and a five-star General of the Army. His statue was placed in front of Marshall Arch in 1978.

There are several monuments. One honors Claudius Crozet, the first president of the VMI Board of Visitors; another honors the Jackson-Hope Medal donated annually since 1877 to the two VMI graduates with the highest academic achievement; another honors Cinncinatus, a 458 B.C. Italian who first represented the citizen-soldier role, and for whom Cinncinati Medals have been awarded to VMI cadets since 1914 due to their greatest degree and excellence of character and service; another two monuments honor the foundation of two fraternities at VMI in 1865 (the Alpha Tau Omega) and in 1869 (the Sigma Nu); and another honors the "Old Guard Tree" that was on the Parade Ground from 1839 to 1954.

A bas relief honors Lemuel Shepherd, a graduate in the VMI class of 1917 and a four-star general who was Commandant of the U.S. Marine Corps. A memorial plaque between Old Barracks and Shell Hall honors Jonathon Daniels. He was a VMI graduate in 1961, who volunteered at the request of Martin Luther King, Jr. to support African-Americans and was killed in 1965 by a racist in Alabama.

IV.A. Statues and Arches

IV.A.1. Francis H. Smith Statue

The Francis Henne Smith statue is located past the west end of the Parade Ground, directly in front of Smith Hall. The statue was created to honor the first VMI Superintendent, who held that position from 1939 to 1889. The statue was sculptured by Ferruccio Legnaioli, and unveiled on 10 June 1931 in a niche between Jackson Memorial Hall and Nichols Hall on a small plaza with a curving bench on the south. The statue was moved to its present location on 19 October 1979, but the bench remained and was later used as a site for the Shepherd bas relief medallion.

The statue depicts Smith holding in his right hand a diploma and in his left hand a Bible given to every VMI cadet at his graduation. General Smith is dressed in his Prince Albert coat with the three-star Confederate rank of Major General, and with two rows of buttons on the front. Smith is wearing spectacles, as one of his nicknames was "Specs". The Art Commission of Virginia did not want the spectacles because they did not think they were artful. However, the VMI alumni demanded the spectacles. The bronze statue is seven-and-one-half feet in height, and the statue stands on a granite base eight feet tall. The inscription on the base is provided below.

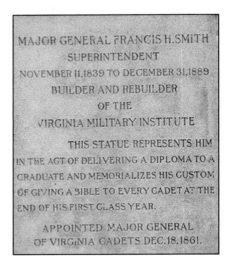

At the 1931 dedication, General Rockenback, a member of the VMI Class of 1889 – the last class to graduate under Smith -- gave a history of General Smith's life and stressed the fact that he was inflexible as far as duty and honor were concerned and iron discipline was imposed to ensure the cadets acted as gentlemen

Serving for fifty years as the first VMI Superintendent from 1839 to 1889, it is obvious that his retirement initiated many discussions about how he should be honored. Surprisingly, no plan developed until 1916, when Greenlee Letcher became involved. He was a member of the VMI Class of 1886 under General Smith and the son of former Virginia Governor John Letcher. As chairman of the VMI Alumni Association years earlier, he had raised the funds for the statue "Virginia Mourning Her Dead", provided by the sculpturer Sir Moses Ezekiel living in Rome. When Greenlee proposed writing a letter to Ezekiel requesting a statue of Superintendent Smith, the VMI alumni immediately supported his proposal. The letter was sent to Ezekiel on 22 June 1916, and Ezekiel responded almost immediately on 18 July 1916, agreeing to make the sculpture.

With Ezekiel's acceptance, Letcher moved boldly forward obtaining advice from B.W. Clinedinst, the painter of the Battle of New Market picture now in Jackson Memorial Hall, and obtaining the approval of Superintendent Edward W. Nichols, the VMI Board of Visitors, the VMI Alumni Association, and General Smith's son Colonel Francis H. Smith, Jr. Letcher then sent to Ezekiel a photograph of General Smith, one of his uniforms, a Bible, and a diploma consistent with Ezekiel's concept of the statue. Unfortunately, before Ezekiel had an opportunity to work on the statue, he died less than a year later on 27 March 1917.

After Ezekiel's death, turmoil was ignited immediately as none of the materials sent to Ezekiel could be found. The selection of a new sculptor was required, and two under consideration were George T. Brewster and Ferruccio Legnaioli. Because the VMI Board of Visitors was somewhat divided in their choice, the Arts Commission of the Commonwealth of Virginia was included in selecting the sculptor. It is incomprehensible that the selection process required 13 years. From the beginning to the end of the effort to obtain the Smith statue, VMI went through three Superintendents starting with Edward W. Nichols, who was succeeded by William H. Cocke in 1924, who was succeeded by John A. Lejeune on 1 July 1929. Finally, the Arts Commission stated it would not choose the sculptor, but would approve or disapprove the choice by the VMI Board of Visitors. Ferruccio Legnaioli was finally selected and approved in the office of Virginia Governor Pollard on 5 September 1930.

Ferruccio Legnaioli had been a Richmond resident since 1890 when he assisted in the construction of what's known today as Old City Hall. Ferruccio Legnaioli was a trained artist from Florence, Italy, who immigrated to New York City in 1902 at the age of 29, born on 20 September 1875, and was associated with the famous architectural firm Legnaioli, McKim, Meade & White. Richmond Businessman Frank Ferrandini, a second-generation Italian-American, brought Legnaioli to Richmond in 1907.

By 1910, Legnaioli created his own studio and employed some 30 people. It is reported that Legnaioli embellished scores of banks, theaters, churches, office buildings and private homes in Richmond, and that his creativity remains part of Richmond's aesthetic appeal. Legnaioli counted his sculpture of the Christopher Columbus statue located in Richmond's Byrd Park among his proudest achievements even though numerous citizens in Richmond decried Columbus as a foreigner, a Roman Catholic, and claimed he was wrongly credited for finding the New World. A Richmond committee made the proposal for the Christopher Columbus statue on 28 May 1925 and, despite the raucous opposition, it was approved and unveiled on 9 December 1927. Legnaioli received the title of Cavalier (Knight) from the Italian King Victor Emmanuel III and the Cross of the Crown, the highest honors possible from his native Italy. He died on 13 January 1958, and was buried in Richmond.

IV.A.2. George C. Marshall Arch and Statue

The George C. Marshall Arch and Statue are located close together. The Marshall Arch named for General George Catlett Marshall, Jr., is the entry to New Barracks which was completed in 1949. The Marshall Statue is located on the east end of the Parade Ground, directly in front of Marshall Arch, and was dedicated on VMI Founders Day, 11 Nov 1978. The statue and arch honor the most distinguished VMI cadet, who graduated in 1901. All information will be provided here about the arch and statue; the biography for Marshall is included in the article Marshall Hall in Section I.

While Marshall Arch was named in 1949, the arch was not dedicated until 15 May 1951 when General Marshall was available to attend. On the same day as the arch dedication, there was obviously the annual New Market Day Ceremony also, and a presentation to General Marshall of the Virginia Distinguished Service Medal. It was also the 50th Reunion for General Marshall and his classmates.

Several thousand friends and admirers were present at the ceremonies dedicating Marshall Arch in tribute to the fifty years of military and statesman service by General Marshall for our country and to the world. Included in this group were top military leaders, and many dignitary U.S. and Virginia government leaders. Bernard Baruch, an American financier, stock investor, statesman, philanthropist, political consultant, and friend and admirer of General Marshall, gave the principal Marshall Arch dedication address.

Governor John S. Battle made the Virginia Distinguished Service Medal presentation to General Marshall in front of the VMI Corps of Cadets on the Parade Ground before the New Market Day ceremony. The Virginia Distinguished Service Medal is given to all Virginia Governors and to officers of the rank of brigadier general or above who command Old Dominion troops in battle. General Marshall qualified for the medal by virtue of his service as Chief of Staff of the United States Army during World War II.

The Marshall statue is the only statue to honor a VMI alumnus and, like the Stonewall Jackson and Washington statues, it stands in front of a Barracks arch which bears his name. The seven-foot bronze statue was sculptured by Augusto Bozzano and stands on an eight-foot base of Santo Tomas stone which rests on a sub-base of the same stone.

In the statue, General Marshall is shown wearing the U. S. Army uniform of the World War II era. Marshall's uniforms, insignia, and all photographic material were sent to Mexico from the Marshall Library to assist Bazzano. The five-star symbol for his General Officer rank and the words "VMI Class of 1901" are incised on the front of the base with his name. Mounted on the back of the base is a bronze plaque which reads: "General of the Army GEORGE CATLETT MARSHALL was born December 31, 1880, at Uniontown, Pennsylvania. After graduating from the Virginia Military Institute in 1901 as First Captain of the Corps of Cadets, he spent fifty years in the active service of his country. He died October 16, 1959, at Washington, D.C., and is buried in the Arlington National Cemetery."

The idea of a Marshall statue covered a long period. For example, Colonel William Couper, a significant VMI historian, expressed his idea in 1939 at the 100th Anniversary of VMI that a statue for General Marshall should be sculpted and placed in front of Barracks. In the 1950 era, the Richmond Chapter of The VMI Alumni Association had a strong interest in a Marshall statue and found a sculptor, Mr. Bryant Baker, but it was not approved. In 1977, VMI's Superintendent General Richard L. Irby recommended, and the Board of Visitors approved, that a statue of General Marshall should be created.

On 11 November 1978, the Marshall statue was unveiled by Marshall's grand-daughter. General Richard L. Irby, the Superintendent and VMI Class of 1939, gave the initial introduction and remarks of welcome. On behalf of VMI, the statue was accepted by Frank G. Louthan, Jr., VMI Class of 1941 and President of the VMI Board of Visitors. Louthan spoke about the greatness of General Marshall and of the sculptor, Senor Augusto Bozzano. Following the acceptance, there was a 19-gun salute executed by the VMI Cadet Battery and a rendition of the "VMI Spirit" by the Regimental Band. It was significant and intentional that the dedication of the statue took place on VMI Founders Day and the dedication took place before a large and enthusiastic crowd on the VMI Parade Ground. The principal address for the statue dedication was made by General Frank McCarthy, VMI Class of 1933, because of his close wartime and peacetime association with General Marshall.

General Lemuel Shepherd, Jr., VMI Class of 1917, another distinguished son of VMI as a former Commandant of the U. S. Marine Corps and Chairman of the Board of Trustees of the VMI Foundation, took the responsibility for acquiring the funds and providing the statue. Speaking at the Marshall Statue dedication, Shepherd praised the efforts of McCarthy as chairman of the fund drive for the statue. General McCarthy served with General Thomas R. Handy, VMI Class of 1914, and Merrill Pasco, VMI Class of 1937, on a fifteen-member committee selected by General Irby. Chairman of the committee was VMI's Dean of the Faculty, General James M. Morgan, Jr., VMI Class of 1945.

Shepherd was also high in his praise for Joseph D. Neikirk, VMI Class of 1932 and vice-president of the VMI Foundation, for his efforts to plan the fund-raising campaign and accomplish the overall project through his Brother Rat Adolfo "Pilo" Ponzanelli, one of the world's great marble industrialists. Ponzanelli was a friend of the sculptor Augusto Bazzano of Mexico, who sculpted the statue. Following approval of the design of the statue by the committee, it required the approval of the Virginia Art Commission and Virginia Governor Mills Godwin.

Because of Augusto Bozzano's esteem for Pilo Ponzanelli and for VMI, he agreed to make the statue of General Marshall for the Institute. Bozzano was internationally famous and 77 years old when he completed the Marshall statue. In addition to the main Marshall statue, Bozzano also made two miniature bronze Marshall statues that were placed in the VMI Museum and the Marshall Library. He had also cast two models of Cincinnatus for the Society of the Cincinnati and one for the VMI Museum before it was decided to have a Cincinnatus Monument instead of a statue. When Bozzano and Ponzanelli had visited VMI and the New Market Battlefield years ago in 1960, Bozzano designed an heroic statue for the New Market Battlefield, which was approved by the Board of Trustees of the VMI Foundation, but was not created because at that time the property did not belong to VMI.

Augusto Bozzano was born in Pietresanta (Toscano), Italy. His father and teacher, Antoni Bozzano, was Director of Fine Arts at the University of Rome. Augusto's basic studies of sculpture and architecture were done at the Fine Art School in Pietrasanta. He studied human anatomy at the Institute of Anatomy at the University of Pisa in Italy, and afterwards perfected his knowledge of plastic arts in Florence. As a sculptor, architect, and inventor, Senor Bozzano spent fifty-eight years in intense artistic activity. His work has been internationally acclaimed and many people have called him the Leonardo da Vinci of the twentieth century. His works can be seen in Italy, Brazil, France, Nicaragua, Mexico, Uruguay, and the United States of America. Some of his most famous works are the equestrian and pedestrian statues of Simon Bolivar in Venezuela as well as the statue of General Marshall.

IV.A.3. "STONEWALL" JACKSON ARCH AND STATUE

The Thomas Jonathan "Stonewall" Jackson Statue is located on the east end of the Parade Ground, directly across from Jackson Arch on the west side of Old Barracks. Jackson Arch was built and named in 1896 when the east side of Old Barracks was extended northward to construct the first Jackson Memorial Hall. Incised on a second-floor walkway inside the Jackson Arch entrance is a famous quote from Jackson: "You May Be Whatever You Resolve To Be". Along with that phrase, at the base of the statue, is the inscription: "The Institute will be heard from today." Those words were uttered to Jackson's cavalry leader, Colonel Thomas T. Munford, VMI Class of 1852, as Jackson was surveying his army before the Battle of Chancellorsville. The day of his greatest triumph, 2 May 1863, was the day he was wounded and later died.

Colonel Keith Gibson, VMI Class of 1977 and director of VMI's Museum and historian, has stated that "Ezekiel placed a fused, flaming cannonball at Jackson's feet, symbolic of Jackson's years as an artillery officer, which was his primary area of military command and instruction at VMI before the Civil War. The statue is not a documentary or historical portrayal of Jackson on the battlefield at Chancellorsville. It's heroic imagery." The placement of the statue on the Parade Ground in 1912 didn't happen just because the area offered a convenient, wide-open space. "That's where Jackson did his best teaching," Gibson says. "He was a somewhat awkward professor in the classroom, but when he got out on the Parade Ground and instructed the cadets in artillery drill, that's where he was comfortable, and that's where he was really most knowledgeable because he had personal experience from the Mexican War."

Appropriately flanking the statue are the four six-pounder guns of the old cadet battery used by Jackson in artillery instruction at VMI. Jackson stood near these same guns at the First Manassas battle when he won his nickname "Stonewall". The guns are a reminder that he was a master artillerist.

The Jackson Statue at VMI was unveiled on 19 June 1912 by Anna Jackson Preston, only twenty-two months old, and the great-granddaughter of both General Jackson and John Thomas Lewis Preston. She was held in the arms of her mother, Mrs. Edmund Randolph Preston. The Reverend James P. Smith offered the opening prayer for the dedication and later pronounced the benediction, as Smith had been a member of Jackson's staff and was one of the first to reach Jackson after he received his wound. Approximately, a crowd of 2,000 attended the dedication, including the VMI Corps of Cadets.

General Edward W. Nichols began the introduction for the dedication. The VMI Superintendent's wife was Mary Evelyn Junkin, whose grandfather was brother to the wives of Stonewall Jackson and John T. L. Preston. Presiding at the dedication was General Thomas T. Munford, a cadet in the Class of 1852 when Jackson came to VMI, and who succeeded as the commander of Jackson's cavalry and was with Jackson in his last battle at Chancellorsville. General Munford introduced Colonel R. Preston Chew, VMI Class of 1862. Chew participated in all of Jackson's campaigns until Jackson's death in May 1863; and, despite his youth, Chew was promoted to the chief of the cavalry's guns under General J.E.B. Stuart. Colonel Chew talked about all of Stonewall Jackson's life, with extensive details about his battles. Also attending the dedication was Governor of Virginia, William Hodges Mann.

In 1912, the Jackson Statue replaced the statue of "Virginia Mourning Her Dead", which was erected on that spot in 1903. The Parade Ground at that time was about five feet higher than it is now and, when the Parade Ground was graded and enlarged in 1914, the statue was left on a mound of rock. In 1932, this mound was blasted away after moving the statue about twenty-five feet westward.

The Jackson statue at VMI, is a copy of the original Jackson statue first erected in 1910 at the West Virginia state capitol in Charleston. The United Daughters of the Confederacy in West Virginia had commissioned Sir Moses Ezekiel, then working in Italy, to design the bronze statue to honor soldiers from western Virginia who fought for the Confederacy, and Jackson was born in Clarksburg, Virginia, which is now West Virginia. Ezekiel was a VMI graduate in the Class of 1867, and also the sculptor of "Virginia Mourning Her Dead". The original Jackson Statue was first erected on the old West Virginia Capitol grounds, and moved to the new Capitol Building grounds in 1921.

IV.A.4. George Washington Arch and Statue

The Washington Arch is the entry to Old Barracks on its south side, and was named for George Washington when the south side of Old Barracks started construction in 1850. It does not appear there was a dedication ceremony for this arch. The Washington Statue was cast in Richmond, Virginia, on 23 February 1856 by William James Hubard, delivered to VMI on 2 July 1856, and dedicated the following day. The bronze statue of George Washington is located on the south side of Letcher Avenue, between Washington Arch and Cocke Hall. When dedicated by Governor Henry A. Wise, he referred to Washington as a "citizen-soldier", directly related to the future of VMI cadets. At the dedication ceremony, the Washington Statue had been set up in what is now the courtyard of Old Barracks. The spectators and distinguished guests sat on the stoops of Barracks that had only three sides at that time.   After the dedication, the statue was moved outside Old Barracks through Washington Arch to a terrace where it was intended to overlook cadet barracks. One hundred and fifty years after its delivery, in 2006, Andrew Baxter, founder of the Richmond-based Bronze et al Ltd., a company specializing in professional conservation and restoration of monumental statuary and sculpture, for the first time cleaned and restored the Washington Statue, returning the weathered light green surface to the original statuary brown.

The history for the statue began in 1784, when the Virginia General Assembly commissioned a statue to honor Washington with a "monument of affection and gratitude" and the "finest marble and best workmanship". This occurred after Washington resigned as Commander-in-

Chief of the Continental Army on 23 December 1783 to return to his private life -- following the "citizen-soldier" role -- five years before his oath on 30 April 1789 to become the first President of the United States.   Virginia Governor Benjamin Harrison asked Thomas Jefferson, the United States Minister to France at that time, for sculptor advice. Jefferson recommended Jean Antoine Houdon (1741–1828), considered the greatest sculptor in France and revered throughout Europe.   Houdon accepted the commission from the Virginia General Assembly to create the statue, and visited Mount Vernon in 1785, where Washington modeled for him, sitting for wet clay life models and a plaster life mask. These models served for many Washington statues.   The standing marble figure commissioned by the Virginia General Assembly was delivered in May 1796, delayed due to construction of the Capitol Rotunda in Richmond, Virginia, and the French Revolution. The statue was considered by many to be the best living likeness of Washington, creating a great demand for copies of the statue.

In 1853, the Virginia General Assembly approved a request from William James Hubard to make castings of Houdon's statue to make a statue for the Virginia Military Institute. Significant support for the statue was provided by Superintendent Smith, who saw Washington as the VMI model of "Citizen-Soldier", much like the Roman Emperor Cincinnatus. Hubard, who had painted portraits of General Richardson and Superintendent Smith, was enthusiastic about placing a statue of George Washington at VMI and through his continuing efforts an act was approved by the Virginia Assembly on 8 March 1856, which authorized Governor Wise to contract with Hubbard for a cast of Houdon's statue of Washington. Hubard took castings directly from Houdon's original marble sculpture of Washington, and then made a mould.

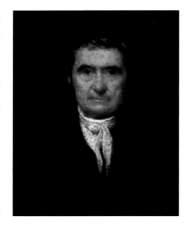

Sculptor William James Hubard (1810–1862) was a British-born artist who began his career as a silhouette portrait cutter, and later worked in Boston and New York as a portrait painter. By mid-century, he was operating a foundry in Richmond for the primary purpose of making bronze statues. Following great difficulties casting the Washington statue, his third attempt was successful in creating the first "Made in USA" bronze statue. The statue is a bronze alloy with a high content of zinc and tin, providing a silvery sheen and making it more resistant to corrosion. The statue was a faithful copy of Houdon's marble statue, and was moved by wagons and horses from Richmond to Lexington, arriving 2 July 1856.

Augmenting Hubard's admiration of VMI, his son William matriculated at VMI, participated in the Battle of New Market, and graduated in the Class of 1865. His grandson Walter Hubard graduated at VMI in 1898, and his great-grandson, Harrison Hubard, graduated from VMI in 1938. Tragically, Hubard was not alive when his son William fought at the Battle of New Market. When Virginia seceded from the Union in April 1861, Hubard, as the owner of one of the few bronze foundries in the Confederacy, began to cast cannons, Brooke rifles, and munitions for the Southern Army. Sculptor Hubard was killed on 15 February 1862, in an explosion at his foundry in Richmond. He was working with John Mercer Brooke to make ammunition for the guns of the Merrimac, a steamer boat first used in the Confederate Navy.

Only eight years after VMI dedicated the Washington Statue, Major General David Hunter led the Union Army into Lexington on 12 June 1864 to burn and destroy all but a few of the VMI buildings. As further punishment, the Washington Statue was "stolen" and taken to Wheeling, Virginia (later to become West Virginia) despite Hunter's order to send it to West Point. Fortunately, after the Civil War ended, Arthur Borman, the first Governor of West Virginia, graciously returned the statue to VMI. The statue was moved from Wheeling, West Virginia to Lynchburg, Virginia on the Baltimore and Ohio Railroad and, from there, it was moved on a canal to Lexington that had been developed by John Jordan. When VMI opened its academic session on 10 September 1866, the Washington statue was rededicated. Former Governor John Letcher gave the principal address as president of the VMI Board of visitors, and Governor F. H. Piermont and General Robert E. Lee were among the distinguished people present, with a very large crowd.

IV.A.5. "Virginia Mourning Her Dead" Statue

The statue of "Virginia Mourning Her Dead" is located on Letcher Avenue, south of the Parade Ground, and directly in front of Nichols Hall. The purpose of the statue was to honor the VMI cadets who perished as a result of the Battle of New Market fought on 15 May 1864. There are markers behind the statue for all the ten cadets who died over a period of six weeks as a result of the wounds received in the battle. The remains of six cadets are buried in a copper box set in the foundation of the statue. The statue was dedicated on Alumni Day, 23 June 1903, following a morning parade and Guard Mount, and placed in front of Old Barracks' Jackson Arch. It was moved in 1912 to its present location when the statue of "Stonewall" Jackson arrived.

The idea for a statue to honor the 10 cadets who passed away as a result of the Battle at New Market came from a lady in Lexington, Miss Margaret W. Freeland. She was president of the New Market Memorial Association formed at the home of Mrs. G. D. Letcher on 28 May 1897, by women desiring to decorate the graves of these VMI cadets. Miss Freeland requested funding support for the monument from Greenlee Davidson Letcher, a VMI member of the Class of 1886, chairman of the VMI Alumni Association, and son of former Virginia Governor John Letcher. When he received the request, Letcher and the VMI alumni immediately supported the proposal and Letcher sent a letter to sculptor Sir Moses Ezekiel in Italy.

Ezekiel was a VMI member of the Class of 1866, and a sergeant in Company "C" at the Battle of New Market. After receiving the request, Ezekiel responded that he already had a statue he named "Virginia Mourning Her Dead", which had been kept in plaster for years. He described the statue as a chainmail clad female figure seated mourning upon a piece of breastwork, her foot resting on a broken cannon overgrown with ivy, and she held a reversed lance in her hands. He added that the statue was bronze and, if placed on the Parade Ground, he would consider it the most appropriate ideal representation of the 10 murdered cadets. VMI accepted Ezekiel's proposal immediately and agreed to have the statue placed on a base with a plaque including all the names of the VMI Corps of Cadets who participated in the Battle of New Market on 15 May 1864. Alumni and VMI friends provided contributions that funded the movement of the statue from Rome to Lexington. A message from Ezekiel in Rome to VMI read, "I am with you, and embracing the threshold of your illustrious portals. Mindful of the past and faithful, I send congratulations. Ezekiel".

Behind the statue are markers as a reminder that ten cadets died as a result of their wounds at the Battle of New Market on 15 May 1864. Five of the cadets --- William Henry Cabell, Charles Gay Crockett, Henry Jenner Jones, William Hugh McDowell, and Jaqueline Beverly Stanard --- died on the battlefield. The sixth, Thomas Garland Jefferson, died three days later in the home of Mrs.  Clinedinst, mother of Benjamin West Clinedinst, who was five years old at the time and was later the artist of "The Battle of New Market" placd in VMI's Jackson Memorial Hall. These six cadets were buried in the Lutheran Church cemetery at New Market. Four other cadets --- Joseph Christopher Wheelwright, Luther Cary Haynes, Alva Curtis Hartsfield, and Samuel Francis Atwill --- died over the period of the next six weeks as a result of the wounds received in battle.

In the spring of 15 May 1866, the remains of five cadets, whose surnames were Jones, McDowell, Jefferson, Wheelwright and Atwill, were brought to VMI for reburial, and initially placed in VMI's Old Hospital. On the second anniversary of the Battle of New Market, five bodies were escorted in a procession of the Corps of Cadets from the VMI Old Hospital to Lexington's Presbyterian Church, where memorial services were held. Following the ceremony, the bodies were placed in a vault in VMI's old Porter's Lodge located near the Limit Gates.

Twelve years later, in 1878, the remains were moved to a newly created cadet cemetery, which no longer exists, located in an area which now is the northwest corner of the VMI Parade Ground. In 1912, when the statue "Virginia Mourning Her Dead" was moved to its present location, the remains of the five cadets were removed from the cadet cemetery and placed in their final graves in a copper box under the statue. The remains of Crockett were added in 1960. The four other cadets who died are buried elsewhere. Cabell's grave is at Hollywood Cemetery in Richmond; Hartsfield is buried in an unmarked grave in Petersburg; Haynes is interred in his cemetery "Sunny Side" in Tappahannock, Virginia; and Stanard is in Orange, Virginia.

IV.A.6 "Spirit of Youth" Statue

The "Spirit of Youth" statue is located south of VMI Barracks in the Memorial Garden in front of Cocke Hall. On 13 June 1939, Mrs. Cocke gave to VMI the white marble statue in memory of her late husband General William Horner Cocke, the fourth VMI Superintendent. The statue was placed and unveiled at the west end of the Memorial Garden toward Jackson Memorial Hall. Robert

Massie, still president of the VMI Board of Visitors since the Memorial Garden was dedicated in 1928, accepted the statue for VMI in front of a distinguished gathering which included Virginia Governor James Price. Massie stated: "With grateful remembrance of the distinguished services rendered his Alma Mater by her husband, I accept from this same woman, as handsome as ever, this splendid gift, set in this lovely garden. It will always be an inspiration to our young men that dwell in these barracks. Surely a noble woman is God's greatest gift to man." The band sounded "The Spirit of VMI" when the ceremony ended.

The statue, 12½ feet high, was executed by the famed sculptor Attilio Piccirilli, who used Corrara marble from Tuscany, Italy. In Piccirilli's biography by Jose Lombardo, it is reported that Piccirilli was inspired to carve the "Spirit of Youth" statue due to the valor of young men who fought and won victories in the battle of World War I, and he accepted the effort to produce the "Spirit of Youth" for VMI because he was so inspired by the valor of VMI cadets at the Battle of New Market.

He was born in Tuscany, Italy in 1866, where his family had been sculptors since the early Renaissance. He came to the United States as a small boy with his family, and they established the Piccirilli sculptural firm in Bronx, New York. Piccirilli became world famous after studying at the academia San Luca in Rome and returning to the United States to sculpture for more than 50 years. His work included the main monument at the entrance of Central Park, a monument for World War I in Albany, New York, the marble "Frageline" in the Metropolitan Museum, the Marconi monument in Washington, DC, and the bust of Thomas Jefferson in the rotunda of the Virginia state capitol in Richmond, Virginia. Piccirilli passed away in 1945.

The "Spirit of Youth" statue was professionally cleaned in 2016 for the first time since it was unveiled in 1939. For years, the statue was under the branches of oak trees, which dropped leaves with tannic acid that created little craters and stains on the statue. The statue was honed by a hand process and has been completely restored. The "Spirit of Youth" stands in front of the east side of Jackson Memorial Hall.

IV.B. Monuments and Memorials

IV.B.1. Crozet Monument and Plaza

The Crozet Plaza, completed in 2011, is directly across Letcher Avenue from Crozet Hall's main entrance. It has been the site of both Claudius Crozet's grave with the monument that stood over his former burial site since 2007. The cast-iron casket containing Crozet's remains were disinterred from in front of Preston Library in order to place his grave to an area across from Crozet Hall with the Crozet Monument.

The Plaza gives Crozet's final resting place greater emphasis and helps draw attention to a significant founder of the Institute. The Plaza consists of a landscaped area surrounding the existing monument, with a bronze relief of Crozet that was added to the monument in 2010.

The footprint of the Plaza uses the shape of the stone archway used at the western entrance of the Blue Ridge Tunnel, a railroad tunnel designed by Crozet. The tunnel was over 4,000 feet in length, the longest tunnel in the United States when completed in 1856, and was opened to railroad traffic in 1858 near Afton Mountain.

Crozet's first grave was at the Shockoe Hill Cemetery in Richmond, Virginia, when he passed away on 29 January 1864. The remains of Claudius Crozet were removed from Richmond in 1942 and reinterred at VMI in front of Preston Library. The ceremony took place on VMI Founders Day, 11 November 1942. When Crozet was buried, the entire Corps of Cadets participated, taps were

sounded, three volleys were fired, and garrison flags were flown at half-staff.

IV.B.2. Daniels Memorial Plaza

The Daniels Memorial Plaza can be visited by walking from Letcher Avenue along a northward 30-foot-wide brick-paved walkway located between Old Barracks and Shell Hall. The Plaza was created in April 2005 to honor Jonathon Myrick Daniels, a VMI graduate in the Class of 1961, who was killed in 1965 as the result of a civil disruption in Alabama.

The dedication ceremony included the unveiling of a plaque with his cadet picture, a quote from Martin Luther King, Jr., a summary of his death, and an accolade from the Episcopal Church. Cabell Brand, VMI Class of 1944, championed the recognition of Daniels and attended the ceremony.

General Lee Badgett, a VMI professor of economics and a classmate of Daniels, and Cadet Andrew Hickman unveiled the plaque. Other guests attending the event included Emily Daniels Robey, Daniels' sister; Richard Morrisoe, who was shot in the incident in which Daniels was killed; Reverend Judith Upham, a colleague of Daniels at the

Episcopal Theological School in Cambridge, Massachusetts; and several other friends. The story below explains his nature and the cause of his death.

His name was used for an arch on the west side of Old Barracks close to the Daniels Plaza for more honor. The arch was named for him in 2004. There is also a Daniels Memorial Library in Scott Shipp Hall dedicated to his memory.

Jonathon Myrick Daniels

Jonathon Myrick Daniels was a native of Keene, New Hampshire, born on 20 March 1939. He graduated as the valedictorian from VMI in the Class of 1961, and was awarded the Danforth Fellowship for post-graduate study and enrolled at Harvard University to study English literature. He left Harvard, however, when he was accepted into the Episcopal Theological School in Cambridge, Massachusetts, and, in 1963, he began his studies to graduate in 1966. In early 1965, Martin Luther King, Jr., was asking that students and clergy come to Selma, Alabama, to participate in a march to the state capital in Montgomery. Daniels and several other  seminary students left for Alabama when they heard King's call. After the Selma March from 7 to 21 March 1965, Civil Rights worker and Episcopal seminarian Daniels and his colleague Judith Upham stayed with the Alonzo West family in Selma, Alabama, deciding to spend the next semester and following summer in Alabama, helping out any way they could. Daniels and Upham tutored children, helped poor locals apply for government aid, and worked to register voters.

On 13 August 1965, Daniels decided to go with a group of people to picket whites-only stores in the small town of Fort Deposit, Alabama. The next day, Daniels and 22 others were arrested for participating in a voter rights demonstration and transferred to the county jail in nearby Hayneville. Shortly after being released on 20 August, Richard Morrisroe, a Catholic priest, and Daniels accompanied two black teenagers, Joyce Bailey and Ruby Sales, to a Hayneville store to buy a soda. They were met at the door by a shotgun-wielding construction worker, Tom Coleman, who was a special county deputy. Coleman threatened the group and then aimed the gun at 16-year-old Ruby Sales. Daniels instantly pushed Sales out of the way and was hit with a full load of buck shot in the chest, killing him instantly, and Morrisroe was also seriously wounded. Coleman was acquitted by a jury of twelve white men, on the grounds of "self-defense". When he heard of the tragedy, Martin Luther King, Jr. said, "One of the most heroic Christian deeds of which I have heard in my entire ministry was performed by Jonathon Daniels."

In the years since his death, Daniels has been recognized in many ways. Two books have been written about his life, and a documentary was produced in 1999. The Episcopal Church added the date of his death to its Calendar of Lesser Feasts and Fasts, and in England's Canterbury Cathedral, Daniels' is listed as a modern day martyr in the Chapel of the Saints and Martyrs of out Time. VMI has also honored Daniels in several ways by naming the library in Scott Shipp Hall as Daniels' Memorial Library, creating a "Jonathon Daniels Humanitarian Award" in 1997, a Daniels Archway on the west side of Old Barracks, and the Daniels Memorial Plaza.

The VMI Board of Visitors voted in 1997 to establish the Jonathon M. Daniels '61 Humanitarian Award. The award emphasizes the virtue of humanitarian public service and recognizes individuals who have made significant personal sacrifices to protect or improve the lives of others. The inaugural presentation of the Jonathon Myrick Daniels '61 Humanitarian Award was given to former President James Earl Carter in 2001, the second award was presented to Ambassador Andrew Young in 2006, the third to Paul V. Hebert (Class of 1968) in 2011, and the fourth to U.S. House of Representative John Lewis in 2015. The Jonathon M. Daniels Humanitarian Award emphasizes the virtue of humanitarian public service and recognizes individuals who have made significant personal sacrifices to protect or improve the lives of others. The award trophy echoes the statue of "Virginia Mourning Her Dead".

IV.B.3. Guard Tree Monument

The "Guard Tree" was a hickory tree that stood on what is now the Parade Ground from the earliest days of the Institute dating to 1839. When VMI started in 1839, there was no Parade Ground. The Institute acquired an additional seven acres west of the old militia barracks for a drill field and a home for Superintendent Smith. Soon the field was doubled with the acquisition of another tract. The drill field was used for camping, drills, and gardens. The Old Guard tree can be seen in this photograph from 1920 at the southeastern corner of the original drill field, with the east side of Old Barracks newly completed in the background.

According to VMI tradition, the hickory tree was called the "Old Guard" tree in the nineteenth century because there was a guard tent under it when cadets camped on the drill field during the summer months. The cadet guard tent had seniority and was set-up in the shade of the only tree. The "Old Guard" tree tradition ended with its death in 1951, when it was reduced to a stump because of disease. The stump was removed in 1954, and replaced with a monument and plaque designed by William M. Simpson. The picture to the left shows the monument that was placed on the Parade Ground with the creator and an unidentified cadet where the "Old Guard" tree was located.

Simpson was a member of the Class of 1924 at VMI, and taught sculpture and painting at VMI. To the right is a picture of the "Old Guard" tree medallion placed on top of the monument.

IV.B.4. Shepherd Bas Relief

The Shepherd Bas Relief is located on a curved bench located south of Letcher Avenue between Jackson Memorial Hall and Nichols Engineering Hall. The bench was initially constructed there in 1931, related to the Francis H. Smith statue which was moved in 1979. The Shepherd Bas Relief was dedicated on 14 May 1981.

The bas relief is a memorial for Lemuel Cornick Shepherd, Jr., who was a four-star general in the U. S. Marine Corps. Bruce Cameron, a member of the VMI Class of 1938 and a member of the VMI Board of Visitors from 1979 to 1988, had expressed his desire in November 1980 to present to VMI a work of art which would depict the service of General Shepherd to his Nation and VMI.

The idea was accepted, and General Shepherd and Cameron commissioned Felixe de Welden, a prominent sculptor from Washington, D.C., to create a bronze bas relief. Welden had known General Shepherd through commissions he had received when General Shepherd was Commandant of the Marine Corps. Welden was a prolific sculptor with many fine arts displayed in this country and abroad. He was Austrian-born and sculptor of the Marine Corps Iwo Jima Memorial in Arlington, Virginia. He was a member of the U.S. Commission of Fine Arts for over 20 years.

The bas relief depicts General Shepherd in a battle dress sitting on the beach in Okinawa as he is planning the capture of the capital, Naha. One of his most prominent efforts was his command of the famed 6th Marine Division in its conquest of Okinawa, a major turning point in the Pacific phase of World War II. The bas relief is a sculpture in which the figures are raised a few inches from a flat background to give a three-dimensional effect. The bas relief term is French for "low relief". The memorial was donated by Bruce Cameron and presented by Vincent Thomas, president of the VMI Board of Visitors and a member of the Class of 1943, to General Shepherd at a luncheon in Moody Hall provided by the Board of Visitors and the VMI Foundation on 14 May 1981. The president of the VMI Foundation also presented Shepherd a resolution from the Board of Trustees expressing their gratitude for his service as chairman of the VMI Foundation's Board of Directors from 1965 until 1981. He was also designated as Chairman Emeritus of the Board of Trustees VMI Foundation.

The picture presents Bruce Cameron, Felixe de Walden, Mrs. Walden, Mrs. Shepherd and Genera Shepherd in Moody Hall on 14 May 1981 at the unveiling of the bas relief.

A portrait had been presented earlier to VMI on 18 December 1958 to honor Shepherd, and was dedicated by General Maxwell D. Taylor, Chief of Staff of the United States Army. The artist was David Silvette, who lived on Richmond's North Side and was the gold standard for institutional, corporate, and society portraits. In 1977, he was commissioned and paid to paint a portrait of Virginia Governor Mills Godwin, Jr. He also had the distinction of painting the only portrait ever done from the life of author F. Scott Fitzgerald, which hangs in the National Portrait Gallery in Washington, D.C. with his other work. The

Shepherd portrait to the right was presented to VMI by Charles Hill Jones, who was General Shepherd's classmate. Mr. Jones was president of the Hershey Creamery Company in Harrisburg, Pennsylvania, and had a farm in Bluemont, Loudoun County, Virginia. The portrait is located in the VMI Admissions Office at 309 Letcher Avenue.

Lemuel Cornick Shepherd, Jr.

Shepard was born on 10 February 1896, in Norfolk, Virginia, and died on 6 August 1990, in La Jolla, California. He was a VMI graduate in the Class of 1917, and was commissioned a second lieutenant in the Marine Corps on 11 April 1917. He was a combat veteran of three wars, including World War I, World War II, and Korea. Shepherd held many of the top jobs in the Marine Corps and earned his fourth star in 1952 when he was named Commandant. He was Commandant from 1952 until 1955 and was the first head of the Marines to serve as a member of the Joint Chiefs of Staff. During that four-year term, he also served as Chairman of the Joint Chiefs of Staff. In addition to the portrait and bas relief, he also received the VMI New Market Medal in 1971, recognizing his qualities of devotion, honor, duty, and leadership.

IV.B.5. Jackson-Hope Monument

The Jackson-Hope Monument is located south of Letcher Avenue between Nichols Engineering Hall and Preston Library. The monument was donated by the family of Stanley Ralph Navas, VMI Class of 1941, and dedicated in 2003. Navas was born on 1 September 1919 in Puerto Rico, joined the U. S. Army after graduation, and earned a Silver Medal in World War II. Later, he was owner of the Navas Pipe Supply Company and died on 18 July 1999 at 79 years of age in Richmond, Virginia.

The monument was built to honor the recipients of the Jackson-Hope Medal, which is presented to cadets at graduation for the highest academic achievement. While the sides of the monument contain bronze plates with the names of the Jackson-Hope Medal recipients, the front of the monument has several interesting words. Near the top of the monument are the expected words "JACKSON-HOPE MEDAL". This shows the medal was named for General "Stonewall" Jackson and an Englishman, Alexander James Beresford Beresford-Hope.

In the middle of the monument face is a replica of the Jackson-Hope Medal, with "Stonewall" Jackson standing and holding his sabre, and the words "JACKSON-HOPE MEDAL" are curved atop the medal. Curving under his feet are the words "THE GIFT OF ENGISH GENTLEMEN" due to the funds donated by English men.

Near the bottom of the monument wall are the words, "IN PACE DECUS IN BELLO PRAESIDIUM", which are included on the back of the medals, recommended by Superintendent Smith. This phrase became the official motto of the Institute adopted by the Board of Visitors on 28 June 1876 at the request of Superintendent Smith, and reaffirmed by the Board of Visitors in 1969. The words are defined as "In Peace a Glorious Asset, In War a Tower of Strength". General Smith's simpler translation was "An ornament in peace, a protection in war." Also on the back of the medals are the words "DISTINGUISHED GRADUATE VIRGINIA MILITARY INSTITUTE" and, on the back of the monument, is stated: "Since 1877, The Jackson-Hope Medals have been bestowed upon the most academically distinguished graduates of Virginia Military Institute."

The first two Jackson-Hope Medals were awarded at VMI graduation by Governor James L. Kemper on 3 Jul 1877 to the first and second most distinguished VMI graduates, Lewis Harvie Strother and Edward Wright Davison. Kemper is pictured to the right.

It is notable that in that period, all the cadets took the same courses of study, so it was uncomplicated to select the two cadets with the best academic achievements. In 1888, the courses began to change between cadets focusing on chemistry, civil engineering and electrical engineering. Over time, the number of cadets grew and new courses were created, but VMI retained the principle of awarding only two Jackson-Hope Medals each year. Examples of the increasing difficulty of selecting the best academic cadets was the addition of a liberal arts course with the class of 1915 and the division of the chemistry course with courses to focus on biology for cadets interested in a medical profession. With the growing number of cadets and courses, the Academic Board and the Board of Visitors recommended to Governor George C. Peery a change in 1935 to increase the number of annual Jackson-Hope Medals from two to four, selecting a cadet from each of the four departments: Chemistry, Civil Engineering, Electrical Engineering, and Liberal Arts. It was also agreed that in case there be no distinguished graduate in either of the four departments, no medals would be awarded that year. The multiple Jackson-Hope Medals were awarded until 1944, when the original idea of only two medals was readopted, and has remained in effect since then.

Beresford-Hope was an Englishman who was born 25 January 1820. His Hope father died in 1831 and his mother married William Carr, Viscount Bereford, which gave him the surname of Beresford-Hope. He graduated from Trinity College in Cambridge in 1837. He was elected to Parliament in 1841, and was there for many years representing different locations and, from 1868 until his death in 1887, he represented the University of Cambridge. His connection to the Jackson-Hope Medals started when he became very concerned about America's Civil War and actually spoke in Parliament advocating recognition of the Confederate States. He was also

chairman of the Southern Independence Association in London and, after the Civil War, led English donors who gave the statue of "Stonewall" Jackson, sculptured by John Henry Foley, to the Commonwealth of Virginia in 1875. It was placed in the Capital Square in Richmond, Virginia. The Englishmen had $1,344.54 remaining from the statue fund and it was sent to Virginia Governor James L. Kemper from Beresford-Hope to be invested in another memorial for "Stonewall" Jackson.

Based on the request for another "Stonewall" Jackson memorial with the funds sent from Beresford-Hope, and the connection between "Stonewall" Jackson and VMI, Governor Kemper, pictured left, sent a letter to Superintendent Smith on 9 May 1876 recommending that "two prizes of gold be engraved and designed as the First Jackson-Hope Medal and Second Jackson-Hope Medal, to be presented annually as rewards of merit to the two most distinguished graduates of the Virginia Military Institute." The Kemper letter recommending the medals was received at VMI on 12 May 1876 and the proposal was immediately referred to the faculty by Superintendent Smith. On the same day, Superintendent Smith wrote to Governor Kemper a letter that "the faculty appreciated the honor and will do all in its power to carry out the instructions of the liberal donors, and to train every class that in each shall be found those upon whom may worthily be conferred the honor of the Jackson-Hope Medals". In his annual report to the VMI Board of Visitors on 20 June 1876, Smith referred to the recommendation of the Academic Board for the medals, and included the design and inscriptions for the medals. Smith submitted the medals' memorial to the General Assembly and a bill was passed in the Virginia Legislature on 6 February 1877, which approved the medals and authorized Governor Kemper to convert the medals fund into State bonds to pay for the Jackson-Hope Medals.

There appear to be several reasons for Governor Kemper's inspiration in creating the Jackson-Hope Medals. He was born on 11 June 1823 at *Mountain Prospect* plantation in Madison County, Virginia, north of Charlottesville. He graduated at 19 years old from Washington College in 1842, and gave the commencement address: "The Need of a Public School System in Virginia". He also attended a few classes at VMI. At that time, VMI and Washington College students could attend classes at the adjacent schools, and all three of the VMI professors – Smith, Preston and Williamson – taught some Washington College students.

After receiving his Master's Degree in 1845, Kemper began to practice law, but volunteered for the U. S. Army in 1846 to fight in the Mexican War. He was discharged from the Army in 1848 and returned to Madison County to practice law. With an interest in politics, Kemper was elected to the Virginia House of Delegates in 1853. He was a strong advocate of state military preparedness and rose to become chairman of the Military Affairs Committee. By 1858, he was a Brigadier General in the Virginia Militia and, in 1861, became speaker of the House of Delegates. Once the Civil War began, Kemper participated in numerous battles as a member of the Confederate Army that included many VMI graduates. At the Battle of Gettysburg, Kemper was wounded by a bullet in the abdomen and thigh, and captured by Union troops. He was exchanged for a Union Army Brigadier General Charles K. Graham on 19 September 1863, and was too ill for more combat. Complications from the inoperable bullet lodged close to a major artery, and eventually paralyzed his left side.

Beginning in 1867, Kemper helped found the Virginia's Conservative Party. In the 1873 election for Governor of Virginia, when the Reconstruction Era ended and former Confederate soldiers regained voting rights, Kemper handily won. Kemper's supporters included former Confederate Generals Jubal Early and Fitzhugh Lee, as well as noted raider John Singleton Mosby. Kemper served as Virginia's Governor from 1 January 1874 to 1 January 1878, and later served on the VMI Board of Visitors again, having been its president in 1865. Kemper died on 7 April 1895 and was buried in the family cemetery in Madison County.

A Jackson-Hope Medals fund, which had been created in 1877 to support the Jackson-Hope Medals, was reconceived extremely in 2001 to establish a "Jackson-Hope Fund" dedicated to increasing VMI academic programs by adding new faculty positions, recognizing distinguished professors, and providing extensive Undergraduate Research. Now, in addition to the Jackson-Hope Medals, the Jackson-Hope Fund grants address strategic initiatives for academic program development, faculty enhancement, and faculty development in technology.

IV.B.6. Cincinnatus Monument

The Cincinnatus Monument is now located south of Letcher Avenue in front of Preston Library. It was first placed between Lejeune Hall and Barracks when it was dedicated on 11 November 1983. The monument was moved to the present location in 2006 when Lejeune Hall was demolished to extend Barracks. VMI Superintendent Sam S. Walker, VMI Class of 1945, presided over the dedication ceremony, and introduced Colonel George M. Brooke, Jr., 1936 VMI graduate and retired professor of history, who was national chairman of the Citizen-Soldier Cincinnatus Monument and Endowment Committee and a member of the Society of the Cincinnati in Virginia. Brooke introduced the principal speaker Catesby B. Jones of Richmond, President General of the Society of the Cincinnati, past president of the Society of the Cincinnati in Virginia, and a member of VMI's Class of 1947. Unveiling the Cincinnatus Monument were Miss Helen Parkhill Murphey, the grand-daughter of Lieutenant General Sumter L. Lowry, a 1914 VMI graduate who was the first recipient of the Cincinnati Medal, and Second Lieutenant Mark D. Jamison, the 1983 Cincinnati Medal winner.

The seven-foot monument of carnelian granite presents a tribute to the Roman patriot Lucius Quinctius Cincinnatus, long recognized as the role-model of a "citizen-soldier" – one of the critical concepts on which VMI was founded in 1839. VMI and the patriotic Society of the Cincinnati have been linked by the citizen-soldier ideal since 1839 when J. T. L. Preston, the Lexington lawyer who championed the founding of the Institute, envisioned the VMI graduates as "fair specimens of citizen-soldiers".

The monument is hexagonal in design, with bronze bas reliefs and plaques mounted to four of its sides. The artist was John Sprotson and the sculptor was Caesar Rufo. The picture on the left is the front of the Cincinnatus Monument. The bas relief depicts the Roman patriot Cincinnatus as he received his battle gear and commission from leaders of the Roman Republic in 458 B.C., and reflects a mural painted in 1859 on a wall in the U.S. Capitol Building in Washington, D.C. Under the bas relief, the name "Cincinnatus" is incised in the granite, and the words "Citizen-Soldier" are incised in the base. The picture on the right shows the back of the monument

which includes plaques that list the names of cadets who were awarded the Cincinnati Medal each year since 1914.

On the right side of the monument is a bas relief of the Society of Cincinnati symbol. In the center of the eagle are three Romans, surrounded by a motto "Omnia reliquit servare rempublicam" which refers to Cincinnatus and means "He relinquished everything to save the Republic." The bas relief also includes the year when The Society of Cincinnati was created in America in 1783 – the year when George Washington resigned as Commander-in-Chief of the Continental Army. In 1913 the Virginia Society established the Society of the Cincinnati Medal at VMI. Below the bas relief is a plaque that provides information about Cincinnatus, the beginning of America's Society of Cincinnati, and the purposes of the Society.

The honor for Lucius Quinctius Cincinnatus was related primarily to his leading the Roman Army in 458 B.C. to defeat Aequi citizens that were attacking Rome. In that period, the Roman Republic consisted of a number of small cities that Rome had decided to govern, and several of the cities were upset by the Roman political control. Aequi had attacked the Romans several times and, when they started their attack in 458 B.C., Cincinnatus, who had been a former Consul, was elected the Roman Dictator by the Senate and left his farm. Cincinnatus recruited every available Roman, led them to Mount Algidus east of Rome, surrounded and defeated the Aequi citizens. Consistent with his attitude, Cincinnatus captured and took the Aequi leaders to

Rome as prisoners, but released all the non-leaders, who returned to Aequi. Sixteen days after the end of the battle, Cincinnatus resigned his dictatorship and returned to his farm. This role led to the term "Citizen-Soldier".

At the conclusion of the American Revolutionary War in 1783, many officers of the Continental Army concluded that they had emulated Cincinnatus. The patriotic, hereditary Society of the Cincinnati was then established in each of the original thirteen colonies and in France. George Washington, the Society's first President General, served from 1783 until his death in 1799. The Virginia Society established the Society of the Cincinnati Medal at VMI in 1913, and since then has generously supported the Institute in many activities as a purpose of the Society.

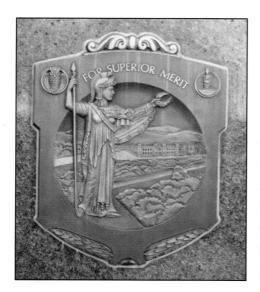

On the left side of the monument appears another bas relief of Cincinnatus with VMI Barracks in the background. It was designed by Moses Ezekiel, and includes a title "FOR SUPERIOR MERIT".

Under this bas relief is a plaque titled "VMI AND THE CITIZEN-SOLDIER" with comments that relate VMI and Citizen-Soldier. At the bottom of the plaque are quotes about VMI and citizen-soldiers, including a quote in 1983 by Lieutenant General Sumter L. Lowry, the first VMI cadet awarded the Cincinnati Medal in 1914. Also included are quotes about VMI from President Franklin D. Roosevelt in 1939, General of the Army George C.

Marshall, VMI '01, in 1945, and Secretary of the Army John O. Marsh, Jr., in 1982.

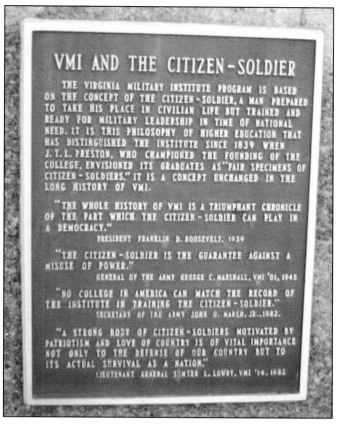

William J. Buchanan, VMI Class of 1950B, did a superb job as chairman of the committee to establish the monument. Other participants included Percy Lincoln, VMI Class of 1957, who was credited with the idea of the monument, and Joseph E. Neikirk, VMI Class of 1932, who was praised for his dedication perseverance, and drive in the successful accomplishment of the entire project. Neikirk also stated that a part of the interest for the Cincinnatus Monument resulted from a book in 1979 by Major General James M. Morgan, Jr., VMI Class of 1945 and former VMI Dean of the Faculty, titled "The Jackson-Hope and the Society of the Cincinati Medals of the Virginia Military Institute: Biographical Sketches of all Recipients, 1877 – 1977".

The committee first considered a seven-foot bronze statue of Cincinnatus as the monument. Two models were cast by Augusto Bazzano of Mexico, who sculptured the Marshall Statue, one for the Society of the Cincinnati and one for the VMI museum. The committee agreed that though the model was superbly done, a symbolic monument was more desired than a statue. The monument was the creation of artist John Sproston of the U.S. Army Institute of Heraldry; the sculptor for the Cincinnatus bas reliefs was Caesar Rufo, a chief sculptor for Roger Williams Mint and a graduate of the Tyler School of Fine Arts at Temple University. Architect Theodore F. Mariani, of Washington, D.C., a 1953 VMI graduate and winner of the Cincinnati Medal, worked with the committee and assisted in the placement of the monument and design of the walkway around it. The granite for the monument and the walkway was provided by the Empire Granite Company of Richmond, Virginia.

The monument should remind each cadet of the importance of his being not only a good and responsible citizen, but a soldier if and when required to serve his country. The monument will remind each cadet the purpose of the Cincinnati Medal and its meaning. There is also an exhibit pertaining to the Cincinnati Medal and the Society of the Cincinnati in the foyer of Preston Library. The Cincinnati Medal has been awarded at VMI each year since 1914 to the graduating cadet who has "demonstrated to the greatest degree of both excellence of character and efficiency of service".

IV.B.7. Alpha Tau Omega and Sigma Nu Monuments

The Alpha Tau Omega (ATΩ) Monument sits on the south side of Letcher Avenue in front of the Preston Library and the Sigma Nu (ΣN) Monument sits on the north side of Letcher Avenue at the southwest corner of the Parade Ground. They commemorate the ATΩ Fraternity founded at VMI on 11 September 1865, and the ΣN Fraternity founded at VMI on 1 January 1869. In 1885, the VMI Board of Visitors ruled that cadets could no longer join fraternities, based on the belief that allegiance to a fraternal group undermined the cohesiveness and loyalty within the Corps of Cadets.

These monuments were placed on the VMI Post in commemoration of both fraternities which were established at VMI and have grown significantly. The ATΩ Monument was dedicated on 20 June 1939. Among the people attending the dedication ceremony was Superintendent Charles E. Kilbourne. The ΣN Monument was dedicated on 25 August 1935. Three hundred delegates who attended the Sigma Nu National Convention held at White Sulphur Springs, West Virginia, visited VMI for the unveiling of the monument. Among the speakers at the commemoration was Superintendent John A. Lejeune.

The ATΩ Fraternity was established in September 1865 by three VMI cadets at a meeting in Richmond, where the VMI cadets were living because the Union Army had destroyed VMI barracks and other buildings in 1864. The leader was Otis Allan Glazebrook, a member of the Class of 1866, who had the thought of creating a fraternal organization of young men with a national character free of prejudice or bias. He had a conversation with Superintendent Smith about establishing a fraternity at VMI and told Smith he did not feel he could imitate a fraternity existing in the north because of the Civil War, and there were no fraternities existing then in the south.

Glazebrook wanted to form a fraternity with the objective for bringing about fraternal relations among all college men in the United States, independent of north and south. He drafted the constitution and rituals for the fraternity, and presented them to two other VMI cadets: Alfred Marshall and Erskine Mayo Ross. They both consented with no changes in the draft of the constitution or the rituals.

After returning to VMI, a selected group of cadets were gathered on 11 September 1865 that considered the outstanding members of their respective classes. They were called together and informed of the fraternal purpose, and agreed with the constitution and rituals. Each cadet made an individual oath and the Mother Chapter of Alpha Tau Omega was formed. The fraternity now has about 250 active and inactive chapters and colonies in the United States, and has initiated more than 250,000 members.

Regarding the Sigma Nu Fraternity, VMI cadets James Frank Hopkins, Greenfield Quarles, and James McIlvaine Riley began their work in October 1868, and were also inspired by Superintendent Smith to create a new fraternity. Before entering VMI in 1866, Hopkins was a Confederate veteran from Arkansas and had experienced tolerating authority during the war. As a result, at VMI he was willing to tolerate a reasonable amount of constraint for the purpose of inducing discipline, but was unwilling to accept any amount of hazing and was adamant about eliminating it. The primary effort of the three cadets to create the Legion of Honor

fraternity was to abolish the environment in which lower class cadets at VMI were suffering from physical harassment and hazing imposed by students in the upper classes.

When the three cadets met on the Parade Ground in October 1868 at a limestone boulder outcropping, later named the "Rock of Sigma Nu", Hopkins, Quarles and Riley clasped hands on a Bible and gave their solemn pledge to form a brotherhood of a new society they called the Legion of Honor. The plaque placed on the monument shows the three cadets with the limestone rock behind them. The original limestone boulder was blasted and destroyed in 1912 when the Parade Ground was being leveled and enlarged. The rock was located 65 yards northwest of the present Sigma Nu Monument. The monument stone was taken from the bed of the Maury River to replicate the original "Sigma Nu Rock".

The Legion of Honor fraternity was publicly founded by the three cadets on 1 January 1869 and publicly named the Sigma Nu (ΣN) Fraternity. The founders encouraged cadet participation and, by the end of 1869, there were fifty knights in the ΣN Fraternity. Hopkins was the leader of the group, and his knowledge of freemasonry was evidenced in the rituals and constitution of the fraternity. The fraternity meetings were generally held one evening each week beside the large limestone boulder. In addition, the house built by the first VMI Post Surgeon, Dr. Robert L. Madison in 1867, also served as a meeting place for the ΣN Fraternity. It is now located at 309 Letcher Avenue.

Since its founding, the ΣN Fraternity has added more than 279 active and inactive chapters and colonies across the United States and Canada, and has initiated more than 225,000 members.

The fraternity's values are summarized as an adherence to the principles of love, honor, and truth. Because of its military heritage, ΣN retains many military elements in its chapter ranks and traditions, and places principal importance on the concept of personal honor.